ULTIMATE FIGHTING TECHNIQUES

Can you win fighting from the bottom against a bigger opponent? Royce applies his defensive fighting skills against the massive (484 lbs) "Akebono" December 31, 2004 K1 Premium Dynamite, Tokyo, Japan. Photo courtesy FEG

BRAZILIAN JIU-JITSU

ULTIMATE FIGHTING TECHNIQUES

Volume 2: Fighting From the Bottom

Royce Gracie

with
Kid Peligro

INVISIBLE CITIES PRESS • MONTPELIER, VERMONT

Invisible Cities Press
41 Northfield Street
Montpelier, VT 05602
www.invisiblecitiespress.com

Library of Congress Cataloging-in-Publication Data
available from Invisible Cities Press

ISBN-13: 978-1-931229-44-9

Anyone practicing the techniques in this book does so at his or her own risk. The
authors and the publisher assume no responsibility for the use or misuse of infor-
mation contained in this book or for any injuries that may occur as a result of
practicing the techniques contained herein. The illustrations and text are for
informational purposes only. It is imperative to practice these holds and techniques under the strict supervision of a qualified instructor. Additionally, one
should consult a physician before embarking on any demanding physical activity.

Printed in the United States of America

Book design by Peter Holm, Sterling Hill Productions
Edited by Tia McCarthy and Carmine Grimaldi, Invisible Cities Press

CONTENTS

INTRODUCTION

In *Ultimate Fighting Techniques Volume I: The Top Game* we discussed many of the important aspects of Gracie Jiu-Jitsu, including its philosophy, training, injuries, positional hierarchy, fundamentals and the belt structure. While we will not go over these topics again in detail, it will be helpful to repeat some of them. For the most part, here in Volume II we will concentrate on the importance of "fighting from the bottom" and the elements that are necessary not only to survive but also to succeed from a seemingly precarious situation.

As Royce says, "No one *wants* to fight from the bottom, I don't! I want to fight from the top. It is, however, unrealistic to imagine that anyone can dictate how he is going to fight when he faces an opponent who is bigger, heavier and stronger. The only thing that can help you survive and eventually win a confrontation like that is your technique and your ability to protect yourself from a seemingly 'bad' position such as being on the bottom."

While modern Mixed Martial Arts fighting was first revolutionized by Royce's win in Ultimate Fighting Championship I, Royce's win over Dan Severn on December 16, 1994, at the finals of U.F.C. IV, best demonstrated Gracie Jiu-Jitsu's effectiveness and efficiency in winning from the bottom. In this fight, Royce—a slender 176 pounds—stayed pinned under the massive 250 pound Greco-Roman wrestler for almost sixteen minutes. Royce was not only able to protect himself from Severn's attempted strikes, but he was also able to submit Severn with the then unknown "triangle choke". From that moment on everyone realized the immense power that Gracie Jiu-Jitsu offered a regular human being!

Gracie Jiu-Jitsu Philosophy

In *Volume I* we explained the Gracie Jiu-Jitsu philosophy. This is so important, especially when fighting from the bottom, that it bears repeating here.

Gracie Jiu-Jitsu is a martial art that works on the principle of action and reaction. This is the beauty of the art; rather than fight against force, a Gracie Jiu-Jitsu practitioner learns to use the opponent's power against him. You know that if you push someone they will push back and if you pull someone they will pull back. So if you want your opponent to come to you, why not push them slightly? When he reacts against the push, then you have him where you want him. That is action and reaction. If you want to pry an opponent's arm away from his body, try pushing the arm against his body. He will react by trying to extend the arm, and that is exactly what you wanted in the first place. Gracie Jiu-Jitsu is based on this simple idea: action-reaction, leverage and base.

Imagine a head-on attack against a powerful fortress—a big mistake in most cases. Now imagine sending a small group to the front to get attention, while sneaking an assault force around the blind side! That is what jiu-jitsu is about: cunning, intelligence, and surprise. Jiu-jitsu is a chess game with your body, in which you use every element available to defeat your opponent. You need to use your arms, legs, fingers, feet and toes, vision, mind, intelligence, sense of touch, and hearing—everything you have—because you are not fighting against a machine but rather against the greatest fighting device ever created—another human being!

Using this action-reaction principle is more important than knowing a thousand techniques without understanding why they work. While beginners believe that they will progress if they learn more techniques, the reality of Gracie Jiu-Jitsu is that you do not need to have a vast array of techniques in your arsenal. What you need to have is a solid foundation of techniques that you know very well and are able to use properly. It is more important to understand how and when to use a certain technique than to know several different attacks for the same position. That is why it takes a lot of time on the mat for a person to advance in Gracie Jiu-Jitsu.

Jiu-jitsu is not like a cake recipe with well-defined, step-by-step instructions. Instead, it involves thousands of different possibilities to each sequence of moves. As you learn more and more moves, little by little, and if you are training with a reasonable amount of awareness and good instruction, you and your body will naturally find what works for you and what should be your game. Different body types should have different arsenals. A tall person with long legs, for instance, will play the closed guard very well and have a good triangle. A person with short legs, on the other hand, may have a much better open guard and guard replacement, but his triangle may not be as effective. A strong and bulky person may be able to control from the top better, but will most likely leave more spaces for escapes than a smaller person.

When learning jiu-jitsu, at every stage (especially the initial ones) the goal is to learn many moves—but don't be obsessed with the idea that progress is measured by the number of moves that you know. Many great fighters are very successful with a small array of moves. This is because they do them so well and are able to select the proper weapons for each situation. In jiu-jitsu it is much better to be a master of few trades rather than a jack of all! If you look at Royce's performances in various NHB matches, you will notce that he used very few "advanced" or "sophisticated" moves. He used the basic moves of Gracie Jiu-Jitsu (most of which are shown in this book) to defeat opponents that were bigger and more powerful than him.

Today, too many fighters are obsessed with fancy moves and never learn the basics. At a tournament recently, a white belt was using a very sophisticated guard and giving his opponent a hard time. But it turned out that it was the only move he knew. Once the guy on top passed his guard, he quickly mounted and submitted the white belt. Many of today's fighters have skipped over the basics and proceeded to advanced moves. That isn't a problem if they fight mirror images of themselves, but when they face more complete fighters, their weaknesses are glaring. How else can you explain the fact that many advanced competitors fall for the most basic chokes and armlocks?

Don't worry about learning many new moves. Instead, practice and understand the moves you do know to the point that they are "in your blood," as Royce likes to say.

Fighting from the bottom: Strategy

Gracie Jiu-Jitsu is primarily an art of self-defense. It gives a smaller, less fit person a chance to defend himself and survive an attack by a bigger, stronger person. The art teaches you that the perfect defense allows you to rest, remain calm and conserve energy while your opponent wastes his energy on unsuccessful attacks. Patience gives a smaller person opportunities to either escape or even attack and submit his assailant or opponent. It's true that most of the principles of fighting from the top apply in most fighting situations, but when you are on the bottom, there are additional sets of requirements you need to succeed since there are greater demands on you when you are in such a precarious position.

The strategy for fighting from the bottom breaks down into the following parts:

- Protect yourself at all times
- Look for a comfortable position
- Keep your wits
- Learn when a position is lost
- Learn when to retreat

- Search for weaknesses in your opponent's position
- Improve your position
- Escape
- Attack and submit

Protect yourself at all times

The number one rule when fighting from the bottom is to protect yourself at all times. First and foremost, you need to protect yourself from being struck (if you are in a street fight or MMA fight) and protect yourself from being submitted (figures A and B). Before you even attempt to escape, counterattack or evade any position, you need to deny your opponent any opportunities to harm you. Patience and good technique will go a long way in helping you here, but the truth is that unless you can protect yourself, your chances of winning the fight are very small at best.

Think about it. When you are on the bottom your opponent has the weight and positional advantage. His mistakes may not be as critical if you can't capitalize on them because of your position. Your mistakes, on the other hand, are amplified. If you find an opening and punch up, hitting your opponent in the face, you will not have much power or weight behind your punch. However, if you fail to protect yourself when he punches down on you with all his weight behind the punch you may be knocked out!

Always look to protect yourself first, even at the risk of not advancing your position. Royce's father, Grandmaster Helio Gracie, wisely says: "If you don't lose, you win!" When you fight someone bigger and stronger than you, if you survive, you are the victor!

Remember that Royce became famous not only by fighting and beating bigger people but also by fighting multiple opponents in the same night. He says, "When you have to fight several times in a night, you *have* to be able to conserve your energy and not get hit." When you protect yourself from your opponent's attacks you gain two rewards: First, as you become more confident in your ability to protect and defend yourself, you will be more relaxed and able to think more clearly than if you are always stressing and struggling. Second, as you foil your opponent's attacks, he will become frustrated and, most importantly, he will get tired. His efforts to attack are more demanding than your efforts to defend; eventually, you will be fresher than him, both mentally and physically. Think about it: If you know you can rely on your defense, you will have a great edge over your opponent. You can be sure that no matter what he does, it will always end in a stalemate. On the other hand, as your opponent wastes more and more energy on fruitless attacks, he will get tired and eventually want to give up!

Look for a comfortable position

In order to survive even for a short time against a stronger and bigger opponent, you need to be in a comfortable position. If you are not comfortable, you will struggle more, get exasperated and expend too much energy. You may even give your opponent the openings for him to finish you.

Although it seems like a simple idea, it is not always easy to find a comfortable position in a fight. After all, there is an opponent on top of you, pressuring you with his weight and trying to look for an opening to either strike (MMA) or catch a submission (MMA and sports match).

In this book we present neutral and comfortable defensive positions for various common situations. As a general rule, keep your limbs close to your body and try not to lie with your back flat on the ground. If you do find yourself in an uncomfortable position, rather than use your arms to push the opponent away, try to quickly bump several times using quick bridging motions (called "upas") (figure D). They will help you take your opponent out of his position and create space for you to adjust and move whatever part of your body is stuck in a bad place. Now remember, these short bumps have a purpose. Use them to create space and ruin your opponent's perfect posture, but do not resort to flopping like a fish and bumping aimlessly. This will just cause you to lose energy and get frustrated.

Keep your wits

Keeping your wits is essential to successfully surviving when faced with adversity. That is true both in life and in martial arts. If you allow yourself to get desperate and lose control, you will not make the best decisions or look for solid solutions to problems. It is a lot easier to remain calm if you protect yourself at all times and stay in a good, comfortable defensive position. But sometimes you may not be able to achieve those goals and may end up, even temporarily, in dangerous situations. That is when it is most important to be able to remain calm and think clearly.

How do you develop this trait? There are specific training exercises that will help you with this. You can do controlled specific position training in which you cannot escape a tough position but only protect yourself. If your partner catches you, you start the drill over. This is probably the worst situation you can place yourself in because you are limiting your options to

protection only. By being in a position that you can only defend you give your opponent free rein; he can try any submission and any variation he wants without worrying about your escape. You can also limit yourself to only a few defensive options; this will greatly increase the stress that you are under. By repeatedly putting yourself under stressful situations, you will start getting used to them and naturally learn to relax and cope. You will think: "I've been here before, I know what to do. I know I can protect myself!" After some time, once you've been successful with your techniques, you will develop confidence in your escapes, increasing your ability to think even more clearly.

Once you are able to protect yourself well, a good drill is to start with the same position, but this time try to escape it. Again, if he catches you or if you escape, start over. Since you allow yourself the "luxury" of escaping, you make your partner's job more difficult and you also learn to coordinate your defense with your escape movements. Although this drill may seem easier than the previous one, it really isn't. Many times, when you try to escape, you will end up forgetting about the proper defense and give an opening for a finish. Keep in mind that defense is always first and escaping is second!

Going one step further with this process, you can try real sparring and place yourself into difficult positions. The reality of the sparring session will add extra zest to your training. Your opponent will be trying harder and the pressure he will apply will definitely be different from the controlled drills that you've done before, but if you really want to learn to relax, this is a great way to improve that skill.

Remember that in these cases you greatly increase the chance that you will have to submit. This may be hard to accept and you may want to give up, but don't let your ego get in the way of your progress. It is better to "tap" many times in practice than to get caught in a real life situation.

Learn when a position is lost

It is easy to underestimate the importance of learning when a position is lost. But understanding when a position is lost means you can immediately start to transition to the next best option instead of continuing to struggle to keep what is already gone. For example, if your opponent is about to break open your guard, you can try keeping your feet locked and waste time and energy and allow your opponent to set up his next move or you can realize the futility of the struggle and instead switch to your next best option, such as preparing a scissor sweep (figures F, G and H) or going to open guard (figure E).

E

F    **G**    **H**

By understanding when a position is lost you can get ahead in the game and gain milliseconds that will count later in the match. Another bonus is that you limit your energy exertion and greatly diminish your frustration. Instead of thinking of it as a loss, recognize it as part of a complete game and an opportunity to adjust and even advance to a better option.

Learn when to retreat

Understanding when it is best to retreat is similar to knowing when a position is lost. It will yield great dividends in your quest to improve and become a complete fighter. Instead of wasting physical and mental energy struggling to advance or maintain a bad position, retreating is often the best solution. Say your opponent has opened your guard and is about to pass. Perhaps you are not quite set up for the sweep you'd like to use but you're almost there. You can risk it all and keep struggling for the sweep, knowing if you fail you allow your opponent an easier path to your side. Or you can retreat and re-lock your legs around him for closed guard. Then you can re-group and start over from a neutral position.

Taking risks is a part of life. But taking *unnecessary* risks will yield positions and put you in a more precarious situation. If you see that all the required elements for a certain move are not there, it is better to retreat and start over than to take the leap and fall.

Search for spaces and weaknesses in your opponent's position

Royce says, "Everyone makes mistakes during a fight or a sports match—the winner is generally the one who makes the fewest mistakes and takes advantage of the opportunities that are given to him by his opponent." At the highest levels, these mistakes can be few and far between,

especially if the opponent is comfortable and not being prodded or tested. You must also look for weaknesses in your opponent's positions. These weaknesses take various forms. They can be spaces that your opponent leaves as he transitions from one position to another. They can be the lack of speed in his transitions. Or perhaps he doesn't keep his balance during his some of his transitions.

Royce also says, "Although I like to protect myself and preserve my energy, I also believe that you can't just lay there passively forever. You need to see if there are kinks in your opponent's armor so you can attack him!" But how do you do that?

First, you need to be alert to opportunities as your opponent moves around during normal positional exchanges as the fight or sparring session progresses. Try to prod his positions to find out how he reacts. For example, if he mounts you, you can do a little bump or upa early on and see how he keeps his balance. If he loses his balance easily, it shouldn't be that difficult to escape with an upa. If he spreads out and opens his legs and arms to brace and gain balance, then you should focus on an elbow escape (figures I, J and K) or hip escape instead. But sometimes you need to make opportunities happen. Say he is in your closed guard. If you don't do anything, he will just gather himself and search for his favorite posture and way to open the guard and proceed from there. Try instead to pull him forward or backwards with your legs. See how he reacts. Reach up with your hand and grab his collar and watch what he does. Does he lean back? Does he worry about protecting his neck from a choke? Take note and use the appropriate option when you see an opening!

Improve your position

Another key to fighting from the bottom is to always look to improve your position. This does not mean that you should abandon the "learn when to retreat" rule, but you should always be looking for opportunities to improve your situation. Obviously, you don't want to lose any gains that you've achieved. In Gracie Jiu-Jitsu, where you fight for every inch and where minute advancements can make all the difference, it is especially important to conserve your gains and try to minimize the possibility of setbacks. This is even more true when you fight from bad positions. But small gains will pay big dividends. They will give you security and a mental boost from knowing that you are going in the right direction. Your opponent will feel that his control is slipping, adding more pressure on him to move and adjust, and giving you greater opportunities for advancement.

Escape

As you improve your position you should always have a clear objective. When fighting from a difficult situation, your main objective of course is surviving; your second objective should always be escaping. Although this may seem obvious it is easy to forget. Many times, you will concentrate so much on surviving that you'll lose sight of trying to escape! If you just defend forever without any attempt at escaping, your opponent will be more and more comfortable with his situation and take bigger chances knowing that you are not looking for the exit door. It is when you combine great defense with escape attempts that you start to wreak havoc on your opponent's position and in his mind. Now he has to deal with many problems at once. He has to deal with the fact that his attacks are not succeeding. He has to cope with his increased frustration at the futility of his efforts. He also knows that soon enough you are going to escape the position and he will have lost what he fought so hard for. The extra pressure will do nothing but make him overreact and give you even more chances to escape.

Attack and submit

Fighting from the bottom is not just about surviving and escaping. It is also about counter-attacking and submitting your opponent. When you develop your abilities to defend and escape to a confident level, you will also see your attacking game improve. Why is that? Because when you have confidence in your defense, you can relax and dedicate some of your thoughts and actions to attacking your opponent's mistakes. It's like when you first start driving, or even better, when playing video games. At first you can't even see what is happening. There are so many things coming at you at once that you keep getting blasted right away. As you learn and adjust and get more used to the situation, you start seeing everything more clearly, and the pieces start moving slowly. It is not because the game speed is turned down. No, it is because you are familiar with the situations and know what to expect and how to react. In jiu-jitsu, once you are confident in your defense and your ability to dodge the bullets, you start seeing when and where you can fire back. Of course this does not happen overnight. But it is guaranteed that as your defensive and escaping skills improve, your attacks will follow until you get to

the point where the defense is so automatic that it appears that all you have to deal with is attacking a slow moving adversary.

For example, when you are confident in your ability to escape the mount, as you escape you will see openings to attack and submit your opponent before you have even completely escaped (figures L, M and N). Imagine, a fighting machine that has complete confidence in his defensive skills, no fear of any position, and is so automatic that it seems that he can concentrate 100% on counter-attacks and submissions. That will be you if you follow these instructions and develop your bottom game to the highest levels.

Now let's move on to the tools you'll need to become a great fighter and address many of the most important techniques for surviving and winning when fighting from the bottom.

Positional Hierarchy

In *Volume I* we discussed the Gracie Jiu-Jitsu positional hierarchy and it bears repeating as we will address these situations in this volume and how to best deal with them. Here is a list of the main positions, from worst to best:

- Opponent is on your back
- Opponent is mounted on you
- Opponent has side-control
- Opponent is on top in your half-guard
- Opponent is in your guard
- You are in his guard
- You are on top in his half-guard
- You have side-control
- You are mounted on your opponent
- You have taken his back

In *Volume I: The Top Game* we dealt with the last five parts of the general hierarchy. Here in *Volume II: Fighting From the Bottom* we will deal with the first five and also knee on the stomach, starting from worst to best.

MEET THE TEAM

The Authors

Royce Gracie

Royce Gracie shocked the world when he entered the Ultimate Fighting Championship in 1993 as an unknown and defeated much larger opponents in record time. He went on to win two more UFCs and many other events. In doing so, he introduced America to Gracie Jiu-Jitsu, now the most in-demand martial art in the world. Royce's stamina is legendary. The result of natural ability and his unique training program, it has allowed him to achieve superhuman feats, including being the only person in no-holds-barred fighting history to defeat four opponents in a single night, and fighting the longest match in modern no-holds-barred history—a 90-minute marathon at the Tokyo Dome in 2002 in front of 90,000 spectators. Royce trains top-level martial artists at his Southern California academy, teaches international seminars, and continues to fight professionally. He is the author of three bestsellers: *Brazilian Jiu-Jitsu Self-Defense Techniques, Superfit* and *Ultimate Fighting Techniques Volume I.*

Kid Peligro

One of the leading martial arts writers in the world, Kid Peligro is responsible for regular columns in *Bodyguard* and *Gracie Magazine,* as well as one of the most widely read Internet MMA news pages, *ADCC News.* He has been the author or coauthor of an unprecedented string of bestsellers in recent years, including *The Gracie Way, Brazilian Jiu-Jitsu: Theory and Technique, Brazilian Jiu-Jitsu Self-Defense Techniques, Brazilian Jiu-Jitsu Black Belt Techniques, Brazilian Jiu-Jitsu Submission Grappling Techniques,* and *Ultimate Fighting Techniques Volume I.* A black belt in jiu-jitsu, Kid's broad involvement in the martial arts has led him to travel to the four corners of the Earth as an ambassador for the sport that changed his life. He makes his home in San Diego.

The Advisors

Pedro and Guilherme Valente were born into the Gracie Jiu-Jitsu tradition. Their father is a seventh-degree black and red belt who holds the title of Master in Gracie Jiu-Jitsu. At age three, Pedro and Gui were already taking private lessons from Grandmaster Helio Gracie. Growing up, the Valente brothers trained daily at the original Gracie Academy in Rio de Janeiro under Helio, Royler, and Rolker Gracie. Pedro stared teaching Gracie Jiu-Jitsu in Miami in the 1990s. With the help of Rorion and Royce Gracie, he founded a Jiu-Jitsu club at the University of Miami. With his brother Gui, he opened the Gracie Miami Jiu-Jitsu Academy a few years later. The brothers' excellent instructional skills, combined with their technical fighting styles, allowed them to receive their black belts directly from grandmaster Helio Gracie. The brothers currently own one of the largest and most successful Gracie Jiu-Jitsu schools in the nation. Furthermore, Pedro holds a masters degree in Business Administration from the University of Miami and Gui holds a degree in Sport Management from Barry University.

BACK POSITION

There is no worse position in a street fight or a sports match than having someone on your back. Your opponent has all the elements to punish and finish you, and you cannot easily see what he is doing, slowing your reactions — a huge disadvantage. At this moment calmness, clear thinking and knowledge of the proper escape techniques are imperative. If you get exasperated or make a mistake the consequences in most cases are dear, even final. When you have someone on your back, proper posture and attention to the defense are your first concerns. Protect yourself at all times, especially your neck. Do not take risks or sacrifice good defense in order to improve your position to escape as a good opponent will take advantage and finish you.

Defend, defend and defend are the keys. Once you are sure of your defense you can move towards improving your position and start your escape action.

1. Back mount face down escape 1

There is no worse position to be in during a fight or a sports match than facing down having your opponent on your back with hooks. From there you have no vision of what your opponent's movements are and he can strike you at will. Royce demonstrates a solid and extremely effective way to escape such a dire situation.

1 Royce is facing down with Pedro mounted on his back with hooks on.

2 Royce escapes one leg first. He kicks the left leg back to release the hook and brings it flat, sliding the knee on the ground. Royce straightens the arm on the same side as the freed leg so one side of his body is flat on the ground. Royce's head presses against that arm to block Pedro's hand from getting a hold on the collar.

2 *Reverse* Notice how Royce keeps his left side flat on the ground.

3 Royce starts to turn to his right until he is on his side. Once there, Royce brings his left elbow in front of Pedro's right thigh and starts the elbow escape. Royce coils the leg in so his thigh touches his elbow.

4 Royce loops the right leg over Pedro's right heel to trap the leg. He plants the right foot on the mat and pushes off it to move his hips to the left and slip the left leg under Pedro's right leg. Notice how Royce keeps the right hand next to the left side of his head to block Pedro from reaching his collar. Also notice how Royce's right foot still traps Pedro's right leg – otherwise Pedro will just step back over and reach the mount.

5 Royce continues his escape by moving his hips further to the left and bringing the right knee in front of Pedro's hips. He then moves the hips back in and replaces the guard.

5 *Reverse* Notice how Royce uses his right elbow in front of Pedro's left thigh to block it and let him bring his right knee in front of it.

2. Back mount face down escape 2

A similar situation is when the opponent has your back with hooks and you are facing down but you are able to get to your knees. This is slightly less dangerous than the previous situation because the opponent has no grip on you, but still requires good technique to escape.

1 Royce is on all fours with Pedro on his back with hooks on.

2 Royce grabs Pedro's right arm. Royce brings his head to the outside of Pedro's right arm so Pedro can no longer choke him.

3 Royce kicks his left leg out (opposite side to the arm he controls) and brings it back with the knee in to release the hook.

4 Royce then pulls Pedro's right arm down, causing him to roll over his right shoulder. As he falls to the ground Royce continues pulling the arm and drives his chest over Pedro's chest until he reaches side control.

Reverse View: **A** Royce grabs Pedro's right arm and slips his head to the outside. **B & C** He then kicks the left leg back and brings it in between Pedro's legs. **D & E** Royce pulls Pedro's right arm, causing him to fall over, and reaches side control.

3. Back mount face down escape 3

At times when faced with the previous situation your opponent allows you to stand up. Perhaps he is slow to attack or doesn't keep enough pressure on your back with his chest. Whatever the case, use this escape. Notice it may be difficult to stand up if your opponent is very heavy or much bigger than you – if that is the case, then use the previous escape. Again the opponent's hands are not grabbing anything.

1 Royce is on all fours with Pedro on his back with hooks on.

2 Before Pedro tries to flatten him down, Royce stands up. He opens the left leg out and plants the foot on the mat. Pushing off it he raises his hips and gets to all fours with hands and feet on the mat. Royce keeps his head low and chin tucked in to prevent the choke. Pedro keeps his hands on the mat so he doesn't slide forward.

3 Royce then uses a similar motion to the previous technique to escape. He grabs Pedro's right arm, slips his head to the outside of it, and pulls it down to force Pedro to fall over his right shoulder.

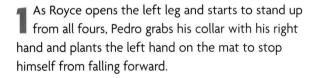

4. Back mount face down escape 4

Many times when you start to stand up from all fours a smart opponent will use one of his hands to grab your gi and try to prevent you from pulling him over. Royce has another option for just that situation.

1 As Royce opens the left leg and starts to stand up from all fours, Pedro grabs his collar with his right hand and plants the left hand on the mat to stop himself from falling forward.

2 Royce needs to free the hook on the same side of the grip. In this case Royce kicks the right leg up and back bringing the knee between Pedro's legs. Pedro has little stability and leans to the left. The only thing stopping him from falling to that side is his left arm posted on the ground.

3 Royce grabs Pedro's left arm with his hands and pulls it down to cause Pedro to fall over his left shoulder.

5. Back escape 1: Slide escape

Another form of the back control situation is shown here. In this case you face up with the opponent on your back. This is a less dire situation than when facing down but you are still extremely vulnerable because you are unable to see your opponent's actions. In the next few techniques, Royce demonstrates a series of back escapes for different situations. In this first case the attacker Pedro grips Royce's collar.

1 Pedro is on Royce's back with his hooks on. Royce's hips face up. Pedro's left hand grabs Royce's right collar as he tries to set up a choke. Royce always wants to escape in the direction that the first attacking hand points out to (in this case Pedro's left hand points towards the right). As his escape is to his right, Royce makes sure his head is to the right side of Pedro's head. Royce wraps his right arm around the top of his head to prevent Pedro from switching hands and counter his escape. Royce's left hand protects his collar as well – should Pedro try to reach with the right hand, Royce can grab it with his left hand, as he does here.

2 Pushing off his feet, Royce drops his head and torso to his right until his back and head are on the ground. At this point Royce can release the right arm from the top of the head as Pedro can no longer reach around it to grab the collar. It is very important for Royce to keep his weight on top of Pedro's right thigh and for him to keep his head and torso straight instead of curling the body in. Otherwise his weight moves towards his buttocks which makes it easy for Pedro to use his right leg and drive Royce back to center and regain back control. Royce continues pushing off his feet and sliding the back on the ground until his body is on Pedro's right side.

3 At this point Royce can either slide to the side and take side control or, if Pedro tries to transition to the mount by looping the left leg over Royce, Royce can use his hands to grab and block Pedro's left leg (the top leg) to prevent him from mounting. Royce keeps his left foot hooked on Pedro's right leg. Royce can either replace the guard by looping his legs around Pedro's body and locking closed guard or, if Pedro continues to insist on coming over the left leg, he can go for this sweep.

4 Pedro comes over the top. Royce directs his left leg to the center so his right foot hooks under the thigh.

5 Royce kicks the right leg up and throws Pedro's left leg over. As he starts to fall, Royce plants his right foot and pushes off to bridge to his left. He ends up on top of Pedro in his guard.

6. Back escape 2

At times during the slide escape your opponent may try blocking your escape route by moving his hips out and forcing you back in with his legs. In that case, as shown here when Pedro over-commits to one side, Royce simply takes what he is given and goes to the other side. We pick up the technique from when Royce is dropping his torso to the right.

1 Royce starts the slide escape to his right by pushing off his feet as he tries dropping his torso to the right.

2 Pedro blocks Royce's escape by pushing off his right foot and escaping his hips to the right to prevent Royce from putting his back on the ground.

3 Royce grabs Pedro's left arm with both hands and loops his right leg over the top of Pedro's left leg ending up face down on Pedro's right side.

4 Royce pulls Pedro's left shoulder with his right hand, keeping Pedro from following him and looping the right leg over his back. Royce keeps pulling on Pedro's left shoulder and drives his head on his chest. Royce pushes off his feet as he continues driving his head and torso forward over Pedro's chest. He slides his left knee over Pedro's left leg until he reaches side control on his left side.

Reverse view: **A, B, C** As Pedro over-commits to the right, Royce loops the right leg over to his left ending up on Pedro's left side on all fours. **D & E** Royce places his left hand in front of Pedro's left thigh and slides his left knee over Pedro's left thigh to prevent him from locking the legs around Royce's left leg and gaining half-guard. Royce pulls Pedro flat on the ground by using his right hand to pull Pedro's left shoulder and slides the left knee over Pedro's left leg to gain side control. Notice how Royce's left hand works in perfect conjunction with his left knee slide to block Pedro from getting half-guard.

7. Back control 1: Opponent crosses his feet

Although crossing your feet when you have someone's back is a cardinal sin, it happens more often than you might imagine even with experience fighters. Be on the look out for this mistake and take advantage of it.

1 Pedro has Royce's back but makes a mistake and crosses his feet. Royce has good defensive posture and sees the mistake.

2 Since Pedro's right foot is over the left, Royce grabs his own right ankle (same side of Pedro's top foot) and pulls his right leg over Pedro's right foot.

3 Royce loops the left leg over his right foot making sure his knee is over the ankle to lock the figure-4 over Pedro's feet. Royce pushes his elbows in against the side of his thighs to trap them in place and force the forearms down on the thighs. Royce extends his body by pushing the hips up to secure the foot-lock. The trapping of the thighs with the elbows adds a lot of pressure to the foot-lock as it keeps Pedro's legs extended. It also prevents him from releasing his feet.

8. Back control 2:
Opponent tries for the rear naked choke

Many times in a fight you are too slow to react and let your opponent get ahead of you. This is especially true under duress situations like having an opponent on your back. Of course keeping
calm even under the worst circumstances will greatly help you
succeed in surviving and escaping any situation. In this case your
opponent has your back with hooks on and starts a rear naked
choke.

1 Pedro has Royce's back and starts to apply a rear
naked choke with his right arm wrapped around
Royce's neck, the hand locked on to his left biceps.
Pedro tries to secure the lock by bending the left arm
and bringing the hand behind Royce's head. It is imperative that Royce defend the choke before Pedro locks
the second hand behind his head.

2 Royce reaches with both hands and grabs Pedro's left
hand. Note: Always grab the top hand with both
hands, preferably with one hand on the wrist and one
hand on the fingers.

3 Royce pulls Pedro's hand to the left side of his head, bringing the arm down over his left shoulder. Royce raises his left elbow to keep Pedro's arm from sliding over the shoulder. Royce pulls Pedro's arm down. He makes sure he twists the wrist so Pedro's elbow faces up. Pulling the wrist down forces the elbow joint for the arm-lock.

3 *Side view*: Check out how Royce controls Pedro's wrist so the elbow faces up.

9. Back control 3:
Opponent has a figure-4 body lock

The figure-4 body lock from back control is a terrific controlling position and very hard to escape. When your opponent is on your back and has his legs locked around your waist, he has all the possibilities and little to worry about, except that Royce has the perfect solution for this seemingly unsolvable problem.

1 Pedro has back control on Royce. His left leg is around Royce's waist and the right leg is locked over the left foot for the figure-4 body-lock. Royce has good defensive posture as his first worry is protecting his neck from a choke. Royce has his hands on the outside of the neck ready to intercept Pedro's hands if he attacks.

2 Pedro attacks with the right arm. Royce traps the wrist using his left hand to pull it down. Royce loops his right leg over Pedro's right foot and pushes off his feet to fall to the right side (opposite side of the leg locking in front of your waist). Royce still protects his neck with both hands as he pulls Pedro's wrist down.

3 Royce slides his right knee as far down towards Pedro's right foot as possible, preferably locking the back of his knee over the foot. Royce's left forearm presses down on Pedro's left thigh and his right forearm holds Pedro's right knee in place. Royce pushes off his feet and extends his hips up, pushing Pedro's left leg up for the foot-lock on the left foot. Notice that Pedro's own right leg applies the pressure on his left foot.

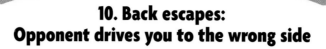

10. Back escapes:
Opponent drives you to the wrong side

At times you cannot escape to the correct side quickly enough and end up on the wrong side for the back escape (away from the direction the hand points to). Although this is not the best situation (he'd prefer an earlier escape to the proper direction), Royce still has a solution to the problem.

1 Pedro has Royce's back with hooks. He grips Royce's left collar with the right hand and pulls him towards the left. Royce's first concern is to stop Pedro's second hand (left hand) from grabbing his collar and completing the choke. He grabs Pedro's left wrist with both hands and locks his left forearm over Pedro's arm to trap it in place.

2 While still holding Pedro's left wrist with his left hand, Royce reaches up with his right arm around the top of his head and grabs Pedro's gi above the right shoulder. Royce pushes off his feet and bridges and directs his head towards the ground.

3 Royce grabs Pedro's right shoulder with the right hand as well.

4 Royce drops off his bridge while he extends his arms to force his body down. He slides his head over Pedro's arm until it escapes under the arm and the head touches the mat. Notice that the key to this escape is for Royce to first bridge up so his head almost touches the ground above Pedro's arm. Then, as he extends the arms, he pushes the body down with his arms and pulls the body down with his legs so his head goes over Pedro's arm and comes down in front of it.

5 Royce continues pushing off his arms and legs and turns to his right into Pedro, ending up in his guard. Always escape in the direction that the hand grabbing the collar points.

MOUNTED POSITION

There are few positions in a fight worse than being mounted by your opponent. Imagine a big opponent with his bodyweight on top of your chest, legs straddling your waist and arms cocked ready to either punch your face or choke you—it is not a pretty picture. The ability to protect yourself from being hit and escaping the position are some of the most important things you can learn in Gracie Jiu-Jitsu. The general rule in Gracie Jiu-Jitsu is: Protect yourself first and escape the position second. In the next few techniques Royce demonstrates a variety of escapes to various mounted situations.

11. Mount posture

It is very important to understand and achieve proper defensive posture when mounted. Proper posture will maximize your escape and defense options. Royce here shows the incorrect and the proper posture.

Royce's arms are loose and the elbows are allowing a more to mount very high (towards Royce's head and away from the hips) thereby taking away the power of Royce's hips to execute a bridge.

Royce's legs are semi-extended with no real purpose or power.

Royce's forearms are up, exposing the arms for a key-lock.

His hands are wide and do not protect the collar and the face.

A: Mount incorrect

Royce's hands are on the collar protecting them and stopping Pedro from securing a proper grab for a choke. If this were a street fight or an NHB match Royce's arms would be bent with the forearms and hands up in front of his face to protect it from punches.

Royce's elbows are tight against his sides. The elbows stop Pedro from moving up and mounting high. If he tries to do so he will have his legs over Royce's arms, allowing Royce to easily escape with an elbow escape.

Royce's left leg is bent and flat on the ground forcing Pedro's leg and foot open and making his mount less effective.

Royce's head, back and butt press down on the ground.

B: Mount correct

12. Mount escapes: Upa

In this first case Pedro has a traditional mount. From here he can either attempt a choke or try to punch. Royce demonstrates the upa or bridge and roll escape.

1 Pedro is mounted on Royce in a normal stance: his knee is tight against Royce's side and the torso is straight above Royce's chest. His right hand pushes down on Royce's throat and the left arm is cocked, hand in a fist ready to punch Royce's face. Note if this were a Gracie Jiu-Jitsu match Pedro's right hand would be grabbing Royce's collar in preparation for the choke. Regardless of whether this is a fight or a sports match the escape is the same. Royce uses his hands in front of his face to protect it from Pedro's punches and loops the left foot over Pedro's right leg (the same side as the hand controlling the neck or the collar).

2 Seeing that Pedro has cocked his arm and is ready to punch, Royce bridges up, raising his hips, and grabs Pedro's right wrist with his right hand and the right elbow with his left hand. Notice that by bridging Royce causes Pedro to fall forward. He is forced to stop the punching motion and use the left hand to brace his fall instead. So long as you keep your hips up, your opponent cannot effectively punch you from the mounted position. It is important for Royce to bridge straight up over his head instead of over his right shoulder so he forces Pedro to plant his left hand above the head instead off Royce's left shoulder making it easier for Royce to roll him over.

3 With Pedro's left hand firmly braced on the ground just above his head and having trapped Pedro's right side (arm held in place with his hands and the leg trapped by his left foot) Royce continues the bridging motion over his left shoulder at approximately 45°. Notice that as Royce kicks his right leg over he uses its momentum to add power to the turning motion.

4 Royce ends up on top, inside Pedro's guard. Royce's hands press on top of Pedro's biceps with the elbows pushing down towards his own thighs. Royce's forearms and hands block Pedro's hands from reaching up for a choke or to punch.

13. Elbow escape

In this situation Pedro is mounted on Royce but unlike the previous position he has his arms planted wide above Royce's head. His legs and feet grapevine around Royce's legs and his hips push down. This method of mounting is commonly used to maintain the position and to prepare a choke, but it is not a good position from which to punch the opponent. Since Pedro has his arms braced wide, Royce will have a difficult time rolling him over to the sides. The elbow escape is his best option.

1 Pedro is mounted on Royce. His arms are open wide and the hands are planted above Royce's head. His hips are pressing down on Royce's hips and the legs are wrapped around Royce's legs with the feet hooked over the shin. Royce's hands press against Pedro's biceps to keep control over his arms and defend against any strikes he may attempt (although this is not a good position to punch from Pedro can deliver shoulder strikes to Royce's face).

2 Royce kicks his legs straight to release Pedro's hooks and circles them in. He brings the right foot under his left leg and steps on Pedro's right heel to prevent him from re-hooking it on Royce's leg.

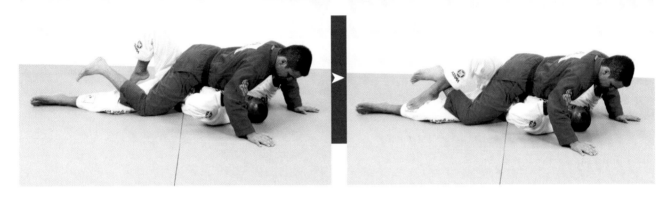

3 Royce then straightens the left leg and drops it flat on the ground. He brings the knee up, sliding it under Pedro's right foot and lifting that leg slightly up. He loops the right leg over to his left and hooks Pedro's right leg with his foot, trapping it between his legs.

4 Royce pulls Pedro's leg to his right with his right foot while at the same time he coils his left leg up and pushes his left arm down so his elbow touches his knee or his thigh to create a barrier. Notice that this barrier prevents Pedro from regaining the mount on that side while at the same time it pushes Pedro's right thigh back.

5 Royce loops the left leg over Pedro's right leg to trap it and release his right foot from that duty so he can push off with it and escape his hips to the left as he extends his left arm up, forcing Pedro's torso to the right.

6 Reversing the view so you can see the rest of the move. Royce loops the left arm under and around Pedro's right arm and holds the triceps. He then brings the right knee up and in front of Pedro's left thigh to form a barrier using the same method of bringing the elbow and knee together.

7 Once his right knee is in front of Pedro's left thigh Royce re-centers his hips. He brings the left leg up on Pedro's back and loops the right foot around Pedro's left thigh to regain full guard. It is very important to understand that it is Royce's hip movement first to the outside left and then back to center that will create the space for his knees and legs to move and regain guard.

14. Mount escape: Bridge and push

A good variation of the mount escape is the bridge and push.. Notice that although it appears that Royce uses his arms to push Pedro away, he actually only uses them to lock the hips in place once he is at the top of the bridging motion. This escape works best when your opponent has his hips away and is not yet set for an attack.

1 Pedro is mounted on Royce. His hips are back and he has yet to begin an attack. Royce holds his hands in front of his face to protect it from punches.

2 Royce plants his hands on Pedro's hips and extends the arms as much as he can. He then pushes off his feet and bridges up while he straightens his torso to force Pedro up. At the top of the bridge Royce's arms are locked and extended, locking Pedro's hips in place.

3 Royce then drops his hips down while turning slightly to his left. He coils his legs in front of Pedro's legs and makes sure his knees are in front of Pedro's thighs.

3 *Opposite* Notice how Royce's hands and arms keep Pedro's hips away so he can get his legs in and the knees in front of Pedro's thighs. Royce hooks the feet under the thighs so he can either kick up and raise Pedro or push off to create space to sit up.

3 *Opposite NHB* If this was an NHB match Royce would quickly get his hands on Pedro's triceps and use the forearms to block Pedro's arms and prevent him from punching.

4 Royce pushes off his leg and slides his hips back creating space for him to sit up. He slides his arms between Pedro's arms and body and locks his hands behind Pedro's back as he buries his head on his chest.

15. Mount escape:
Bridge and push to foot-lock

At times when you apply the hand push your opponent will fall slightly to the side (or you may direct him to the side). If that occurs you can quickly go to this variation of the escape and attack him with a foot-lock.

1 Pedro is mounted on Royce. Royce locks his hands on Pedro's hips as he prepares to bridge and push.

2 Royce bridges up and locks Pedro's hips away with his extended arms. When Royce drops his hips down he falls to his left and Pedro follows him. Royce slides his hips back and kicks the right leg up, pushing Pedro's left leg with his thigh.

3 Royce rolls to his left as he keeps his left knee and shin in front of the hips in between Pedro's legs. This blocks Pedro from coming forward to defend the attack. Royce loops his right leg around Pedro's left leg and locks the foot on his hips. Notice how Royce locks his right arm around Pedro's left leg with the elbow pressing in. This allows him to quickly transition to the foot-lock.

3 *Reverse* Royce places the right foot on Pedro's left hip. The heel comes in and the toes point out. Royce's left foot presses down on Pedro's right calf with the foot hooked on the thigh so he cannot push and try to walk away to escape the attack.

4 Royce continues to roll to his left until he has his chest down on the mat. He slides his right elbow towards Pedro's left foot. He then wraps the arm around the ankle locking his right hand on his collar and places the left hand on Pedro's shin. Royce arches his torso back. This extends Pedro's foot back for the foot-lock. Royce makes sure that the blade of his right forearm presses against Pedro's Achilles tendon.

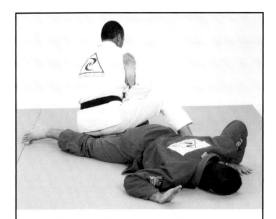

4 *Reverse* Note: for maximum pressure Royce's arm locks around Pedro's leg right at the ankle to trap the foot on his armpit.

5 *Variation* If your opponent doesn't fall to the side, simply push him with your right leg so he falls back and apply the straight foot-lock.

16. Elbow escape variation:
Opponent side mounts

At times when using the elbow escapes or the hip push escape, your opponent will shift his hips and lift his leg to transfer his weight to the side trying to block the escape and switch to the side mount. Here is an escape that deals with that situation.

1 Begin to escape with either the elbow escape or, as shown here, the bridge and push.

2 Pedro tries to counter the escape by planting his hands wide and shifting to the side mount. He drops his weight to his left and raises the right knee.

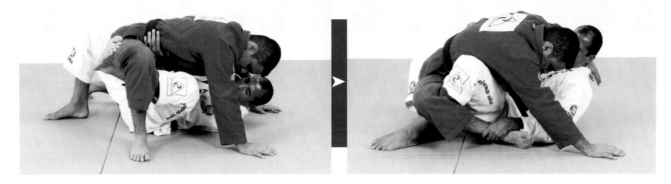

3 Royce continues to hold his left knee high and grabs Pedro's right ankle with his left hand. Royce points the knee forward, driving the shin on Pedro's right knee, while at he same time he pulls Pedro's ankle back to force him to fall backwards for the sweep. Notice that at this point sometimes the opponent will open his left leg out in an attempt to regain his balance. If he does that then immediately attack that leg with the foot-lock as shown in technique 4.

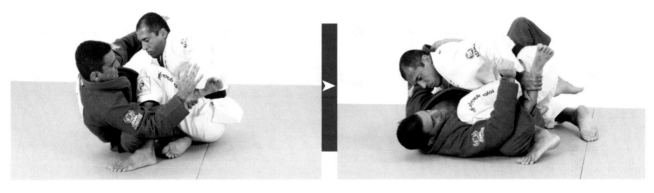

4 Royce sits up and follows Pedro's fall while still pulling the ankle.

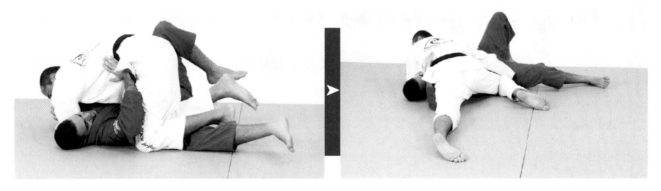

5 Royce kneels with his left knee over Pedro's right thigh making sure to keep the toes on the mat to prevent Pedro from locking his legs around Royce's right leg for half-guard. Royce then slides the right leg over Pedro's right leg and gains side-control.

17. Mount escape: Twist

You can take advantage of your opponent's commitment to punching and surprise him with the twist escape. The key to this escape is timing — surprising your opponent when he is leaning back to punch.

1 Pedro is mounted on Royce and cocks the right hand to punch. Royce has his arms bent with the forearms and hands in front of his face to protect it. Royce turns slightly to his left and drops the left thigh over Pedro's right foot.

2 Royce sits up while turning to his left by propping off his left elbow. He uses the right forearm in front of his face to block Pedro's punches.

3 Royce pushes off his right foot and bridges his hips up and to the left, using an explosive twisting motion to force Pedro to fall to that side. Notice that Royce's left leg on top of Pedro's right leg prevents Pedro from opening the leg out to block the reversal.

4 Royce ends up in Pedro's guard with his hands cupping Pedro's arms to block Pedro's punches.

18. Mounted escape: Opponent hugs the neck

It is quite common for your opponent to hug your head with his arm when mounted on you. He can control your head and limit your escape options, and he may be setting up a choke. Here Royce demonstrates a variation of the upa escape.

1 Pedro is mounted on Royce and wraps the right arm around Royce's head.

2 Royce grabs the outside of Pedro's right arm with his left hand to prevent him from pulling it out. At the same time he loops his left leg over Pedro's right leg and traps the foot with his left foot. Royce now has trapped Pedro's right side. Royce places his right hand on Pedro's left hip and locks the arm tight to maintain the distance and to help with the escape.

3 Royce pushes off his legs and bridges up and to his left over his shoulder, causing Pedro to roll over and end up inside Royce's guard.

2 & 3 *Reverse techniques* Check out how Royce's right hand locks onto Pedro's left hip and helps force the roll over by pushing the hips as he bridges and rolls.

19. Mount escape 2: Opponent's hands on the mat

Another common situation when your opponent is mounted on you is for him to open his arms and plant his hands wide above your head. This is a position of stability for him and although it does not present immediate danger for you, you need to know how to escape it.

1 Pedro is mounted on Royce and has his arms open wide with the hands planted on the mat above Royce's head. Royce elects to attack the right side. He grabs Pedro's right wrist with his left hand.

2 Pushing off his feet, Royce then slides his body up towards Pedro's right wrist so his head touches the arm (Royce may have to wiggle a little for his torso and head to reach up to Pedro's wrist). Royce changes the controlling grip by sliding his left hand up to Pedro's elbow and using the right hand to grab the wrist instead. Royce loops the left leg over Pedro's right leg to lock the left foot on the mat and trap the leg. Notice Royce's elbows are tight against his body for maximum control.

3 Using the same bridge and roll motion as in technique 14, Royce pushes off his feet and turns to his left, taking Pedro with him and ending up in his guard. Again, notice that Royce bridges over his left shoulder and not directly to the left side.

20. Mounted choke defense: Grip variations

Royce shows a variety of grips and the proper defenses in preparation for the upa escape.

A Pedro is mounted on Royce and uses his hands to choke him. Pedro is using a common street-fighting choke with the hands grabbing the throat and the thumbs pressing on the windpipe. Royce grabs Pedro's right wrist with his right hand to push the wrist slightly to the left and release the choke. He uses his left hand to grab Pedro's right triceps and locks the left foot over Pedro's right leg.

B Pedro grabs both collars with his hands. Royce grabs Pedro's right wrist with his right hand. He uses his left hand to grab Pedro's right triceps and locks his left foot over Pedro's right leg.

C Pedro's right hand grabs Royce's right collar. Royce grabs Pedro's right wrist with his right hand and pulls the wrist to his right while bringing his elbow down and tight against his side thus relieving the pressure of the choke. He uses his left hand to grab Pedro's right triceps and locks the left foot over Pedro's right leg.

D Pedro has both hands on the mat next to Royce's head. Royce grabs Pedro's right wrist with his right hand. This time he keeps the elbow up in front of Pedro's chest. Royce will use the elbow to help drive Pedro over as he bridges and rolls. He uses his left hand to grab Pedro's right triceps and locks the left foot over Pedro's right leg.

E Pedro has both hands on Royce's collars. The hands are positioned palm up and grip with the fingers inside the collar and the thumb outside. This is typical of a situation where Pedro would grab Royce's right collar with his right hand and then slide second hand (left hand) under his right arm to grab the collar for the choke. Royce grabs Pedro's wrists and pulls then out as he brings his elbows down and to his side to relieve the choke.

F Pedro grabs Royce's left collar with his left hand (fingers in and thumb out) and attacks by looping the second hand (right hand) over the left arm to grab the right collar with the thumb in and the fingers out. In this case the top hand is the choking hand (the hand that applies the most pressure) so Royce concentrates on it. He grabs Pedro's right wrist with his right hand and pulls it out and down while driving his right elbow down and tight against his body. At the same time he locks his left hand on top of Pedro's forearm and pushes it down and towards his right to relieve the choking pressure.

G Pedro grabs Royce's right collar with his right hand (fingers in and thumb out) and comes over the top with the left hand to grab Royce's left collar (the thumb in and fingers out). Royce intercepts the second hand from gripping his collar. He grabs the bottom of Pedro's left hand with his right hand and pulls it out, twisting the hand.

21. Mount defense:
Choke defense: Arm around the top

A very common way for the mounted opponent to attack your neck with a choke involves him, after securing the first hand grip on your collar, dropping his head to the opposite side to brace and stop your upa escape. From there he will loop his arm around your head until he can grip the other collar. Royce has a solid counter to defuse the attack.

1 Pedro is mounted on Royce with his right hand gripping Royce's right collar (fingers in and thumb out). Royce prepares the counter and sets up an upa escape. He grabs Pedro's right wrist with his right hand and the back of the right elbow with his left hand while trapping Pedro's right foot with his left foot.

2 Sensing the bridge to his right, Pedro drops his head to the left of Royce's head (Pedro's right) using the head to block the upa roll-out. Pedro places his left elbow on the mat and circles it over Royce's head until he can bring it in next to Royce's left ear and grab the collar with his hand. Royce's first counter is to press his face against Pedro's chest to prevent him from sliding the forearm in front of Royce's face to get to the neck and apply the choke.

3 Royce reaches with his right hand and pulls Pedro's left arm back towards his right shoulder. At the same time he drops his head over the top of Pedro's left forearm to trap it and stopping the choke. From here Royce would use the upa escape to his right as shown in technique 12.

3 *Side view* Notice how Royce "hides" his neck by pressing his face on Pedro's chest. As he controls and brings Pedro's left arm back towards his right shoulder, Royce slides his head over Pedro's forearm and uses it to press the forearm down against the mat and trap it.

22. Key-lock defense: Block the hand

The key-lock is a great attack from the mounted position. It is often used in combination with the arm-lock or to attack a stubborn choke defense (as when your hands are blocking the collars). Royce is a firm believer that simple is better and always tries to stop the attack before it fully develops.

1 Pedro is mounted on Royce. Royce has good defense on Pedro's choke attempt by grabbing the hands and pulling them out.

2 Pedro quickly switches to the key-lock. He spins his left hand around and grabs Royce's left wrist. He pushes the wrist out as he tries to slide the right hand under Royce's left triceps and lock it on his left wrist for the figure-4 around Royce's left arm, setting up the key-lock. Royce's first defense is always to intercept and defuse the attack. He pushes off his right foot and turns his torso slightly to his left. This puts his weight on his left elbow and top of the arm, pressing them against the mat and making it impossible for Pedro to slide his right hand under and secure the key-lock. Although it seems too simple a counter, you will be surprised at how effective it is.

2 *Detail* Notice how Royce uses Pedro's attempt to push his wrist down to leverage and further press his elbow against the mat. As he fights Pedro's push on the wrist he braces the elbow on the mat even harder.

23. Mount key-lock defense: Opponent secures the lock

Sometimes your opponent is quicker than you (or your reaction is slow) and he ends up getting ahead of you and securing the lock. If your opponent is able to secure the key-lock this escape will foil his success. The key to this escape is to quickly turn and bridge towards the arm under attack.

1 Pedro secures the key-lock on Royce's left arm. He pushes Royce's wrist down with his left hand and slides the right hand under the arm until he can grab his own left wrist to lock the figure-4 around Royce's left arm and set up the submission.

2 Royce places his right hand on Pedro's left triceps and pushes off his right foot as he turns to the left (the side of the arm under attack).

3 Royce bridges to his left while using his free hand to push Pedro's elbow and force the arm open. He pulls his left arm towards his body and tucks his left elbow in.

3 *Detail* Notice Royce's right hand position: it pushes Pedro's arm up so he can pull and tuck his left elbow in. It is very important for Royce to turn to his left and push Pedro's arm up just prior to the bridging action otherwise he will bridge and his elbow will be stuck pressing down on Pedro's forearm.

4 As he comes down from the bridge Royce further pulls his left arm to release the elbow from the figure-4 and foil the key-lock.

24. Mount defense: Punches

Another variation to defend and escape when the opponent is on top of you punching is presented here. This is a more MMA-specific application. Royce concerns himself the entire time with controlling Pedro's arms and protecting himself from being punched or head-butted.

1 Pedro is mounted on Royce and pulls back his right arm to punch his face.

2 Royce places his hands and forearms in front of his face to protect it from the strikes. Royce pushes off his feet to bridge his hips up, forcing Pedro to fall forward and place his hands on the mat to stop the fall. Notice that as long as Royce has his hips up Pedro cannot effectively pull his arms off the ground and punch.

3 Royce wraps his left arm around Pedro's right arm and hooks the left hand on Pedro's left triceps to prevent him from pulling the arm back for a punch. Royce makes sure to turn his face towards the trapped arm and keep the head close to Pedro's head to avoid head-butts. With Pedro's arm under control and in no danger of being punched, Royce can drop his hips back down. Royce loops his left foot over Pedro's right leg to lock it in place.

4 Royce pushes off his legs to bridge up and over his left shoulder and roll over to his left. At the top of the bridge Royce kicks his right leg over to add to the momentum of the rotation. Royce ends up in Pedro's guard with his hands on the triceps and his forearms blocking Pedro's arms from punching. Royce then raises his head and straightens his back to gain proper posture.

25. Sleeve choke (Ezequiel) defense

The sleeve choke is a very common attack used from the mounted position. Because of its subtlety your opponent will find it especially effective if you are unaware of the imminent attack or if you do not know how to defend it. The defense is very simple as Royce demonstrates here.

1 Pedro is mounted on Royce. His chest is tight against Royce's chest and his right arm is wrapped around Royce's head. Pedro tries to sneak the sleeve choke in by planting the left elbow on the mat. He holds inside his left sleeve with his right hand and makes the left hand into a knife with all fingers tightly together pointing up. Royce has good defensive posture: his hands are in front of his neck above the collar to protect both the neck and the collar.

2 Pedro tries to loop his left hand around and over Royce's head to apply the choke. Royce's right hand blocks it from coming in fully, foiling the attack.

3 Royce slides the left hand to the right, further protecting that side from the sleeve choke.

4 Royce now uses the left hand to block Pedro's left hand from choking him and uses the right hand on Pedro's left biceps to push the arm away.

5 Royce traps Pedro's right arm with his left hand and arm and locks Pedro's right foot with his left foot.

6 Royce does an upa over his left shoulder ending up in Pedro's guard.

26. Amassa-pao
(Thrusting choke defense)

Another very common and surprisingly effective choke from the mount is the "amassa pao" or thrusting choke. In it the attacker grabs and crosses your collars using his body weight to add to the choking pressure. Quick thinking and applying this defense will save you from a tapout!

1 Pedro is mounted on Royce. He holds Royce's right collar with his left hand (fingers in and thumb out so the knuckles point towards Royce's throat) and the left collar with his right hand, setting up the thrusting choke. Pedro drives his left hand down and across Royce's throat, pushing the collar and his knuckles down on Royce's throat. Pedro drops his weight down on his left arm to add more pressure to the choke.

2 Royce quickly turns his shoulders and neck to his left so his Adam's apple is out of the direct choking pressure. He grabs the top of Pedro's left hand with both hands (right hand directly over Pedro's hand and the left hand over his right hand). Royce pulls Pedro's hand back by driving his own elbows to his right side.

3 Royce returns his shoulders to the center and pulls Pedro's hand back with him to release the choke. Be prepared at this point for the opponent to reverse and attack with the thrusting choke to the opposite side by using the right hand to choke.

27. Knuckle choke

The knuckle choke or nut-cracker choke is another one of those surprising effectively and seldom used chokes. Perhaps it is not commonly used because it is easy to defend. However, if you are caught in one and do not know the defense or get surprised by one you may be forced to submit, so learn and master this defense.

1 Pedro is mounted on Royce. He prepares the knuckle choke by grabbing Royce's collars with his hands. Notice Pedro's grip: the fingers are inside and the thumb on the outside pointing down, so his knuckles face Royce's throat. Royce's hands and arms are in a defensive, protective position: hands and forearms in front of his face to protect against both punches and chokes.

1 *Detail* Notice how Royce's hands are always inside of Pedro's arms and in front of his face and collar. This allows him to quickly defend attacks by either blocking or defusing them as they occur.

2 Royce shoots his left arm up and out to deflect Pedro's right arm pressure. Royce's right hand pushes Pedro's left biceps away, taking away any power from the knuckle choke.

3 Royce wraps his left arm around Pedro's right arm and traps it by holding the triceps with his hand. Note: Every time you wrap the arm you need to trap the arm in place so your opponent cannot pull it away. Royce traps Pedro's right leg as well by looping his left foot over it. He then pushes off his feet and bridges over the left shoulder, ending up inside Pedro's guard. Royce has both hands on Pedro's biceps, blocking his arms.

28. Double attack defense

The double attack is a formidable and difficult attack to defend against. The two options force you to divide your attention which gives your opponent the extra edge he needs to get a submission. The key to defending any double attack is to have proper posture and execute exactly the right defense at the right time. Special tip: It is important to keep your back flat on the ground to make it difficult for the opponent to reach the side-mount for the double attack.

1 Pedro is mounted on Royce and grips the right collar with his right hand. Royce grabs Pedro's right wrist with his right hand, pulling it down and away from his throat, and the right elbow with his left hand to execute the upa. Pedro then shifts to the left side-mount, trapping Royce's right elbow with his hips and setting up the double attack by attacking Royce's right arm.

2 Royce's first step in his defense is to keep the right elbow super-tight so Pedro cannot grab the inside of that arm. Second, Royce pushes off the feet and escapes the hips to the left while tucking the right elbow in to protect it and pushing Pedro's right leg (that is up) away. This however exposes Royce's left collar for the choke so the left hand needs to be ready to block Pedro's left hand from grabbing the collar.

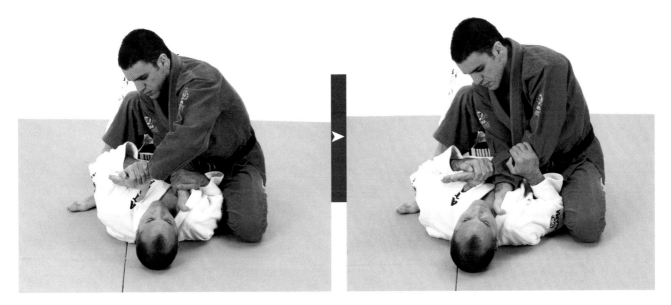

3 As Pedro attempts to grab Royce's collar Royce uses his left hand to grab the bottom part of Pedro's hand, pulling and twisting it out. Having foiled the choke, Royce releases his right hand from Pedro's right wrist and grabs the left forearm at the elbow instead thereby blocking Pedro's left arm and preventing him from pulling it away.

4 Royce continues to push off his feet and turns to his right as he escapes his hips further to the left. This opens Pedro's right leg out and sets up the footlock.

5 Royce continues turning to his right and loops his left leg around Pedro's right leg. He places the left foot on Pedro's right hip and slides his bent left leg between Pedro's legs. Notice how Royce traps Pedro's right foot by pushing his thighs together and by looping his bent left arm over Pedro's shin.

6 Royce extends his left leg to push Pedro away. He has Pedro's right foot trapped under the left armpit in perfect position for the foot-lock.

7 Royce slips the left hand under Pedro's right calf and grabs his own right collar. He then tightens the noose around Pedro's ankle as he props himself on his right elbow. Royce arches his torso back to apply the foot-lock.

7 ***Detail*** Very important: Notice how Royce uses the blade of his forearm to press against Pedro's Achilles. This adds a tremendous amount of pressure to the foot-lock. It creates an excruciating pain and you need much less arch on the foot to reach the submission. Unlike the common foot-lock where the pressure comes from arching the body back to push the toes down and apply pressure on the joint, Royce's technical detail turbo-charges the lock.

29. Mount arm-lock defense

As you know Royce is always looking to defend and avoid any attacks *before* they get set. As he likes to say, "If you let them get the lock, many times the only escape is to tap!" But at times you may not react quickly enough or even sense the imminent danger to stop an attack until it is fully developed. In this case, the arm-lock from the mount, the opponent is able to secure control of your arm and set up the arm-lock. Although it is always better to get the early escape and avoid having to use last options, this escape when properly applied will save you from having to submit.

1 Pedro has set up the arm-lock as he attacks Royce's right arm. Pedro's right arm is wrapped around Royce's right arm and tries to pry it open while his legs over Royce's head and chest prevent Royce from rolling over the top. Of course ideally Royce would like to roll to his right and tuck the elbow under Pedro's hips foiling the attack but Pedro has good control with his hips tight against Royce's arm locking the elbow in place. Royce's first step is to protect his arm. His right hand holds the left collar.

2 Royce's left hand pushes Pedro's left leg away thus freeing his head to slip over the leg.

3 Once Royce's head is on top of Pedro's left thigh he presses it down on the leg and bridges up until the back of his head touches the ground. It is very important for Royce to keep his body arched back so his weight is on top of Pedro's thigh instead of tightening up, otherwise Pedro can loop the leg back over the head. It is a very common mistake when using this escape to curl the torso and head forward thus placing the weight on your butt instead of on the attacker's leg which allows him to push off his left foot and escape the hips out and loop the leg over your head again.

4 Royce continues to push off his feet and slides his back over Pedro's thigh until his hips are over the thigh. At this point the arm-lock is fully defended. Pedro will try to turn to his right and mount, so Royce uses the left hand to block Pedro's right leg from coming over and stops the mount. If Pedro persists in his attempt to mount, Royce immediately will use the elbow escape.

5 Royce has two choices. He can either continue to slide his body away until he ends up in side control on Pedro's left side, which Pedro will fight to block, or Royce can turn in. He chooses the second, ending up in Pedro's guard.

SIDE CONTROL

The side control is perhaps the most stable position in an attacker's arsenal. With his chest pressing down on your chest and his legs out and open for balance, the side-control not only ensures his stability but it is also a great position from which to launch many attacks and submission attempts. Being able to protect yourself from the side control, and better yet escape from it, is a must if you are going to survive in a street fight, NHB match or a Gracie Jiu-Jitsu sports match. In the next few techniques Royce will demonstrate escapes and defenses to several circumstances that can occur when faced with an opponent in side control.

30. Side-control defensive posture, correct and incorrect

Good posture is critical at all times especially when you are in an inferior or more vulnerable position. Here Royce demonstrates the correct and incorrect ways to position yourself when in side control.

A Incorrect Royce has incorrect posture. His back is flat on the mat (A), his right arm serves no purpose and simply hugs Pedro (B). Royce's left arm is trapped by Pedro's arms in a position vulnerable for an arm-lock (C).

B Correct Royce is turned to his right side, his back is off the mat (A). Royce's right arm is bent with the elbow and the forearm pressing against and blocking Pedro's left hip (B). Royce's left arm is protected and tucked under Pedro's right armpit, and pushes up slightly to force Pedro off balance (C).

31. Side control escape 1 and Drill

A common side control situation is shown here with Pedro on Royce's right side and both arms on the opposite side. In this case Royce escapes to the side. Pedro does not try to follow Royce's escape by applying pressure with his weight on Royce.

1 Pedro has side control on Royce's right side with his arms on Royce's left side. His left elbow presses against Royce's head and the right elbow is tight against Royce's left hip to prevent him from moving. Pedro's right knee is tight against Royce's right side, preventing him from easily sliding his right knee in and replacing the guard. Royce has good defensive posture with his right arm bent at the elbow and the forearm blocking Pedro's left hip. Royce's left arm is under Pedro's right armpit so it is not exposed for any key-locks or arm-locks. Royce presses the left forearm up to force Pedro slightly off-balance. In most side control situations Royce does not want to have his back flat on the ground so he pushes off his feet and turns to the right side.

2 Royce continues to push with his legs and escapes his hips to the left as he turns his body to his right as he extends his arms to create distance between Pedro's hips and himself. In this case, because of Royce's quick escape and arm position, Pedro doesn't try to close the gap again which allows Royce to continue escaping the hips. He continues spinning to his right until he has turned to his knees and is at 180° in relation to Pedro.

3 Royce slides his left arm around Pedro's left leg until the hand appears on the outside of the leg and he can grab the wrist with his right hand to lock the leg. Notice that Royce's left forearm is behind Pedro's knee and his elbows are pressed tight together. Royce lifts his head up and pushes it against Pedro's left side.

4 Royce pulls his left arm in and brings Pedro's left leg in causing Pedro to fall to his left side. Notice that Royce does not pull the leg towards himself but rather in towards the left. Royce escapes the position and ends up in side control on Pedro's left side. Note: This is a very good drill to practice side control as you end up in the same position where your opponent started so you both can continuously practice the elbow escape.

Reverse View Check out Royce's legwork. He steps out with the left foot and moves his hips around until he is facing Pedro while at the same time extending the arms to create distance between them. Also notice how Royce pulls Pedro's left leg in towards his left causing him to fall to the side.

32. Side control escape 2

This time around as Royce begins his side control escape Pedro applies his weight to press Royce's back flat to the mat. Royce simply follows Pedro's pressure, falls back and replaces the guard.

1 As Royce gets to his knees Pedro extends his legs and pushes back on Royce. He drops his weight on Royce's shoulders making it difficult for Royce to use the previous technique.

2 Royce steps out and forward with his left leg while still keeping his right knee on the mat and the leg open.

3 Royce yields to Pedro's forward pressure and sits down on the mat. He drops the right leg to the ground and makes sure the knee is outside Pedro's left thigh.

4 Royce continues to sit back. Notice that Royce's head naturally comes out under Pedro's left arm so he pushes it back. This forces Pedro to his right and makes it easier for Royce to slide his right leg around Pedro's body. As he sits back Royce slides his arms inside Pedro's arms. He loops his legs around Pedro's body and locks them on the back to regain full guard. Notice that Pedro is quick to loop his left arm over Royce's head to prevent him from going to his back. Royce grabs Pedro's triceps with his hands while using the forearms to block the arms from punching.

33. Side control escape 3

This case is a variation of the previous technique. As Royce begins to sit back and replace the guard, Pedro continues to hug Royce's back to try to pull him forward but he fails to bring the left arm to Royce's right side. Royce takes advantage of Pedro's mistake and goes to his back. We pick up at the point where Royce starts to sit down.

1 In the previous technique sequence Royce begins to sit back down and tries to replace the guard but Pedro fights him. He uses his arms to try to pull Royce's back forward and prevent him from dropping his back to the ground. Because of this, Pedro fails to swing his left arm to Royce's right side of the head and exposes his back.

2 Royce kicks his head back. He pushes against Pedro's left triceps and forces him to his (Royce's) left, exposing the back.

3 Royce continues to drive his head back pressing it against Pedro's shoulder so he can't loop the arm back over the head. He slides his body to his right as he loops the right arm around Pedro's back. Royce grabs Pedro's right armpit with his right hand and uses it to help pull himself over the top of Pedro.

4 Royce continues pulling himself over Pedro's back. Pedro struggles to get up and regain posture by propping his knees. Royce puts his left foot on Pedro's right knee and pushes it, causing Pedro to fall. This makes it easier for Royce to loop the right leg over and lock the heel of that foot in front of Pedro's right hips thereby securing the second hook and taking the back. Notice that Royce's left foot hook was already in place as he came around.

Reverse view Check out how Royce pushing off his left leg and kicking the head back against Pedro's left triceps causes Pedro to move to the right and makes it easy for Royce to take the back. Also notice how Royce uses his left foot to push Pedro's right knee and open the space for the right foot to hook in front of Pedro's right hip.

34. Side-control escape 4

Here, Royce tries to push off and escape the hips to turn to all fours. Pedro sprawls in response, opening his legs and pushing forward with his chest. Rather than fight to use the first escape Royce once again takes advantage of what is presented. Now that Pedro's right knee is back because of the sprawl there is space for Royce to slide his right knee in front of Pedro's hips and proceed to replace the guard.

1 Pedro has side control on Royce's right side. Both his arms are on Royce's left side. When Royce tries to push and escape the hips to the left Pedro sprawls and drive his chest forward against Royce's chest. Royce has good posture with his right arm bent and the forearm in front of Pedro's left hip and the left arm tucked under Pedro's right armpit.

2 Since Pedro's knees are back now it becomes very easy for Royce to replace the guard. He turns to his right and coils the right leg back so his right knee comes in front of Pedro's hips.

3 Royce pushes off his left leg and moves his hips back to center while at the same time he extends the right forearm to push and lock Pedro's left hip away. Royce continues to move his hips to the right until his right knee emerges on Pedro's left side. At this point Royce has regained guard.

4 Royce continues to escape the hips to the right so he can hook the right leg around Pedro's left leg and loop it around the back. He then locks his feet on Pedro's back for closed guard. Royce makes sure his hands block Pedro's arms.

Front view Notice how Royce opens his left leg back and pushes off his left foot to turn to the right. He escapes the hips slightly left so he can bring the right knee in front of Pedro's hips. He then pushes off the same foot to drive his hips back in and replace the guard.

35. Side control escape 5

In this case Pedro's right arm blocks Royce's right hip which stops the right leg from coming in during his attempt to replace the guard. Royce uses a clever move to secure control over Pedro and reverse him.

1 Pedro has side control on Royce's right side. This time, however, his right arm is on opposite side of his left arm, near Royce's right hip and blocking Royce's right knee.

2 Royce pushes off his left leg and bridges to his right as he escapes his hips left. At the same times Royce slides his left arm under Pedro's chest until it comes out on Pedro's left side under the armpit. Royce circles the left arm around Pedro's left arm and under his face and reaches around the back until he can lock his hands together. Notice that Royce traps Pedro's left arm and head with his arms and chest.

3 Royce steps out and back with his left leg and escapes his hips to the left.

4 Royce pushes off his left foot and bridges to his right, rolling Pedro over and ending up in side control himself. Royce's last hip escape is critical. He needs to have the proper body angle in relation to Pedro's body in order to be able to bridge and reverse. Royce needs to be at approximately 45° in relation to Pedro so he can push and roll over the left shoulder.

Opposite view Check out how Royce traps Pedro's left arm with his arms and chest. This clears the way for him to bridge and roll over Pedro's left shoulder.

36. Side control escape 6

When Royce attempts the bridge over the shoulder Pedro blocks the roll by sprawling. Again Royce takes what his opponent gives to him. Pedro, by moving his knees out, creates the space for Royce to simply replace the guard. Royce goes one step further and takes his back. We pick up the technique from the moment Royce traps Pedro's arm and is ready to bridge.

1 Royce has trapped Pedro's left arm as in the previous technique and is ready to bridge and roll over the left shoulder. Sensing the imminent reversal Pedro shoots his legs back and sprawls to stop the roll.

2 With Pedro's right knee away Royce steps out with his left leg and pushes off that foot to escape the hips to the left. This creates the proper angle so he can easily slide the right knee in front of Pedro's hips until they come out on Pedro's left side. At this point Royce has effectively replaced the guard with his right knee and shin in front of Pedro's left leg. Because of the trapped arm Royce sees that he has a clear path to Pedro's back.

3 Royce pushes off his left foot and moves his hips to the right. Pedro cannot stop him because his left arm is trapped.

4 Royce continues moving to his right until he is on Pedro's left side. At this point Royce breaks his hands open and grabs Pedro's left wrist with his right hand to help pull himself around. He then loops the right leg over Pedro's back and props up first on his left elbow and then his hand so he can climb over Pedro's back and hook the heel of his right foot on Pedro's right hip for the back control. Again notice that Royce's left leg is already in position between Pedro's legs, so he can hook it automatically in front of Pedro's left hip.

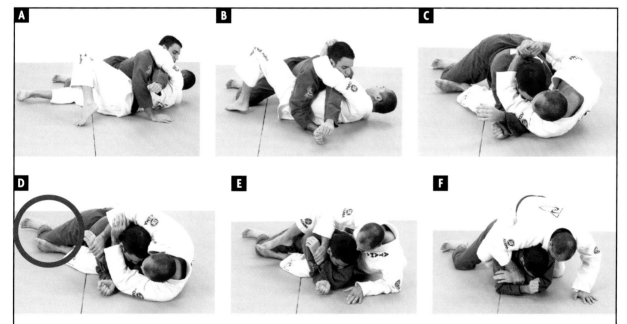

Opposite side view Again observe Royce's legwork as he moves his hips out **(A)** and then in **(B)**. Also notice that once he gets to Pedro's left side **(C & D)**, he switches the lock and grips Pedro's left wrist with his right hand to help pull himself up and over his back **(E)**. Note how Royce's left foot pushes on Pedro's right knee in image **(F)** to create the space for his right foot to hook.

37. Side control: Kimura defense

The "kimura" is a dangerous attack from the side-control. Many times your arm is exposed because of a movement and positional exchanging, making it available for the kimura. It is important to be very aware of the attack and immediately react properly when you sense the opponent reach for the grip.

1 Pedro has side control on Royce's right side. He reaches and grabs Royce's left wrist with his right hand setting up the kimura. He now needs to slide the left hand under Royce's left arm and lock it on his own right wrist for the figure-4.

2 Royce senses the attack and pushes his elbow down to the mat. Royce pushes off his right foot and slightly turns his body to the left to put his bodyweight on the elbow. At the same time he forces the forearm up and uses Pedro's resistance to further add pressure to the elbow and top of the arm. He locks the arm down on the mat to prevent Pedro from sliding the left hand under.

3 If Royce fails to block Pedro's left hand from sliding under his left arm then Pedro will secure the figure-4 for the kimura lock. In that case the defense is far more difficult. Royce would have to bump and turn towards the left side to hide and protect the elbow in a way similar to the key-lock in technique 23.

38. North-south escape 1

The north-south position is normally a transitory position as the opponent switches sides from the side control. The north-south, however, can be used as a controlling position by your opponent and he can even launch some attacks from it. Therefore it is important to learn how to properly break the control and escape from it. In this first case the opponent on the north-south control has his arms inside your arms.

1 Pedro has north-south control over Royce. His arms are inside Royce's arms with his hands grabbing the belt for extra control over Royce's body. Royce has two options that work equally well. If the opponent is wearing a belt (as in a sports match) his hands will grab the belt on one side (in this case, the right side of his hips). If it is a submission wrestling match or an NHB fight and he is not wearing a belt then (as Royce shows here) Royce will make a frame on one side. Royce slides the left arm in front of Pedro's hips so his forearm pushes against the right thigh. Royce completes the frame by using his right hand to grab the left wrist. Royce's legs are out.

2 Royce will make a pendulum with his legs, swinging them hard first towards one side, then the other until he creates enough momentum to break the control. Since his frame is to his right side, he first swings the legs to the right.

3 When Royce feels Pedro's move to mount (pushing off his right leg and looping it over) it is the perfect moment to push off his feet and bridge to his right shoulder. He reaches up with his left arm and reverses Pedro.

3 *Reverse* Notice how Royce's right hand is able to control the hip and slow Pedro's mount attempt. It also helps Royce sense the moment when Pedro tries to loop the right leg for the mount. Also notice how Royce reaches up with his left arm to pushing Pedro's chest back. Royce bridges over his right shoulder (45° angle) and not to the side (90° angle).

4 Depending on how Pedro reacts with his legs, Royce may end up either in the guard or he may slide to the side-control.

41. Side-control to mount defense 2: Back door escape

Another option for your opponent is to simply keep you flat and try to power to the mount by sliding the knee over the belly. Royce has the perfect counter to the attack and not only escapes but takes the back as well.

1 Pedro has side control on Royce's right side. Royce has good defensive posture with his right forearm blocking Pedro's left hip and the left arm under Pedro's right armpit. Pedro starts sliding his right knee over Royce's stomach as he tries to mount.

2 Royce's right forearm plays an important role here as it blocks Pedro's left leg. When Pedro starts to reach the mount his weight is on his head and torso, making his legs very light. Royce realizes this gives him the opportunity to escape through the back door. Royce starts the elbow escape to his right. His right forearm presses against Pedro's left thigh and he brings his right knee up so it touches the elbow to form a block. Royce pushes off his left foot and escapes his hips to the right. He uses the leg and forearm to lift Pedro's left leg and slide his right leg under it until he ends up on Pedro's left side.

3 Royce grabs Pedro's right shoulder (he could also grasp his armpit) and helps pull himself over the top for back control.

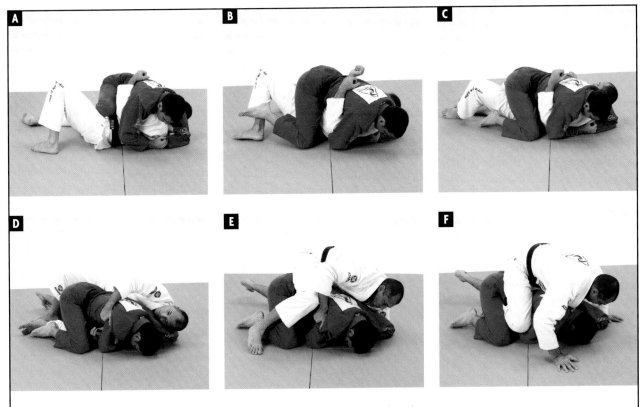

Reverse view A, B & C When Pedro reaches the mount, Royce is already escaping to his back side. ***D & E*** Royce grabs Pedro's right armpit and pulls himself up. ***F*** Royce hooks the right heel on Pedro's right hip for back control.

42. Side-control: Arm-lock defense

A common attack from the side-control is the arm-lock. In your scramble to escape or while defending the pass, your arm may end up exposed. A cagey opponent may take advantage of your mistake and attack the arm by wrapping it for the arm-lock. The key to this escape is timing. You must take advantage of his movement to free your elbow and foil his attack. As he goes around, use the knee on the same side of the arm under attackto push the grip away and break the elbow free.

1 Royce ends up under Pedro with his left arm trapped between Pedro's head and left arm, exposing it for the arm-lock. Pedro adjusts and gets in position for the arm-lock.

2 When Pedro adjusts his body position by moving to his left (clockwise) Royce pushes off his right foot and moves his hips in the same direction, circling away from Pedro and turning his body to his left.

3 As they circle around Royce turns his torso to his left. He pulls the elbow towards the mat as much as possible to counter Pedro's upwards pull.

4 When Pedro fights to pull Royce's arm up to apply the arm-lock, Royce brings his left knee up (same side as the trapped arm) and uses it to push Pedro's left elbow to the left. At the same time Royce pushes off his right foot and turns his shoulder further to the left, yanking the elbow out and releasing Pedro's control over it, thereby escaping the arm-lock.

43. Side-control cross choke defense

The cross choke from side control is a very common and effective attack. If you don't know how to properly defend it you will undoubtedly have to submit. The defense however is simple as Royce demonstrates here.

1 Pedro is on Royce's right side preparing the cross choke. His right arm is wrapped under Royce's right arm, and the hand grabs the collar near Royce's neck. To complete the choke Pedro wants to grab Royce's left collar with his left hand and drive his left elbow down to the mat so his forearm presses on Royce's throat.

2 Anticipation is always the key to any successful defense (or attack, for that matter). Royce recognizes the danger and Pedro's intention as soon as Pedro's right hand grips his collar. Royce's first attempt to defend the choke is to use his left hand to protect his left collar and to block Pedro's left hand from grabbing it. If he fails and Pedro succeeds with the grip, as shown here, Royce then grabs Pedro's left forearm with his left hand to pull it up.

3 Royce pushes off his feet and turns into Pedro so his head gets under and presses up against Pedro's chest. Pedro cannot complete the choke any more as he cannot pass his forearm in front of Royce's face.

4 Royce's left hand pulls Pedro's left elbow open to further defend against Pedro's attack.

44. Side Control:
Head and arm choke escape 1

Many fighters have submitted to the head and arm choke from side control. The position can occur quite easily during a scramble or a cagey opponent can position himself and force you to fall into it. Use one of these two solutions to escape this devastating choke.

1 Pedro has side-control on Royce and traps his right arm and head between his own head and arm. Pedro applies the pressure by pushing off his feet and driving his head against Royce's right arm which pushes against the right side of the neck. At the same time he cinches the right arm in, pressing it against the left side of Royce's neck for the choke. Royce releases the pressure on the right side of his neck by making a frame with the right arm extended and the left hand grabbing the right wrist to push it and the arm to the right.

2 Royce brings his right leg up and grabs the inside of the thigh just under the knee with his right hand. He drives the leg down, further releasing the pressure of his right arm against the neck.

3 Royce opens his left leg and pushes off the foot, rotating his body counter-clockwise until he is at approximately 90° in relation to Pedro.

4 Royce kicks both legs up towards his head and then drives them back down, using the momentum of the pendulum to force Pedro to fall to his back. Royce squares his hips, ending up in side control. Notice that Royce's legs swing first up, then down and then he walks around in a counter-clockwise semi-circle.

45. Side Control:
Head and arm choke escape 2

At times when using the previous escape your opponent will base out and block your leg swing. Use this reversal to escape from the head and arm triangle. Always try the previous escape first; if it doesn't work only then transition to this one.

1 Royce applies the previous escape but as he swings his legs down Pedro opens his left leg way back and blocks the reversal.

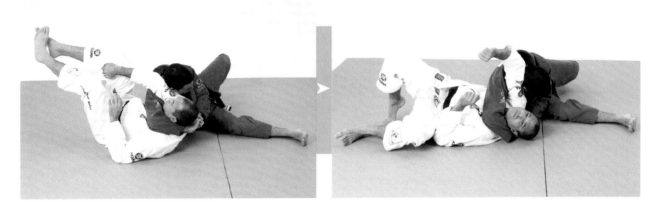

2 As he returns to an almost flat position Royce releases his right hand and breaks his frame. Royce pushes off his right foot and falls to his right while still forcing his right arm towards Pedro's head.

3 Royce pushes further off his right leg and turns over his left shoulder. He shoots the right leg over and turns his body at the same time. He spins his head and arm inside Pedro's trap and ends up on all fours on the right side.

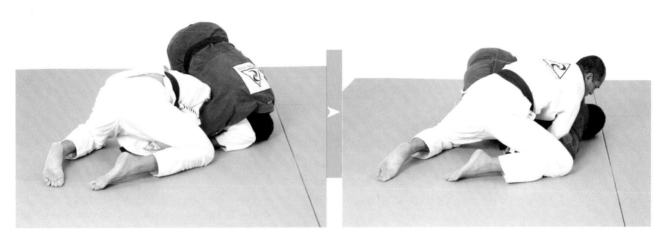

4 Royce's head escapes from Pedro's grip. He ends up
with his chest pressing on Pedro's back.

46. Side-control MMA position 1: Opponent turns hips down

The next series of positions refer to specific MMA/street-fight situations. The most important aspect of the defense is not allowing your opponent to hit you and then, depending on his reaction, escaping the position. Notice that in MMA/street-fight situations Royce does not expose himself in any way in his attempt to escape. He simply gets a good protective posture and waits for the opponent to bring an opportunity to escape.

In this case the attacker is on Royce's right and has both elbows on the same side. He turns clockwise so his hips face down towards Royce's feet, positioning himself to hit with the right hand.

1 Pedro's right elbow is near the hip and the left elbow presses against Royce's left ear. Royce blocks Pedro's strikes by using his left arm to drive up Pedro's right arm. Royce's right forearm, bent at the elbow, touches Pedro's left thigh and blocks his left hip and knee strikes. Royce's right leg is curled in and presses Pedro's right side to block his right knee strikes. Royce's left leg is curled with the thigh almost touching the left elbow. His head is up off the ground with the face close to Pedro's chest so he cannot hit it. Royce stays alert and uses the head pushing against Pedro's left triceps to control the arm so he can't elbow him or wrap the arm around his head.

2 Pedro tries to switch his hips and turn them down so he can hit Royce with his right hand.

3 As soon as Pedro starts to turn Royce pushes off his feet and extends the left arm. He bridges over his right shoulder to force Pedro to fall to his back.

4 Royce ends up in side control.

47. Side-control MMA position 2: Opponent turns hips up

Here Pedro tries to turn to his right (counter-clockwise) so his hips face towards Royce's head allowing him to hit with his left hand.

1 Royce has good defensive position from side control.

2 Pedro turns counter-clockwise. His hips now face Royce's head so he can strike with his left hand. Royce uses his right hand to block the punch – he reaches towards Pedro's left biceps and the hand intercepts the punch. As soon as Pedro turns, Royce pushes off his feet and bridges up over his right shoulder. He extends the left arm up and tucks the right arm in, forcing Pedro forward, and slides to his back.

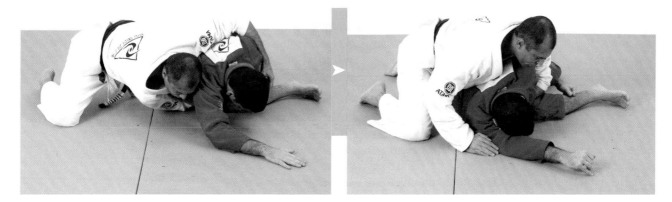

3 Royce continues turning his hips towards the ground, ending up on all fours. Royce ends up behind Pedro. Depending on Pedro's weight distribution and body position Royce can now either take his back or maintain side control.

48. Side-control MMA position 3: Opponent tries knee strikes

Continuing with the defensive blocks from side control MMA, here Royce demonstrates how to properly block if Pedro attempts knee strikes.

A Pedro tries to deliver a left knee strike. Royce blocks the path by reaching out with his left forearm and uses the same bridge and tuck as in technique 34 to escape.

B1 Pedro tries to deliver a right knee strike. Royce takes advantage of the space created by Pedro coiling his leg by bringing his right knee in front of his thigh to block the strike.

B2 Royce continues sliding the right knee in front of Pedro's hips until it comes out on the right side and replaces the guard.

49. Knee on the stomach escape 1

The knee on the stomach is one of the worst and most debilitating positions to be under. Your opponent's knee pressing down on your stomach is akin to being punched, undermining not only your stamina but your willpower as well. Although the knee on the stomach is not a very stable position for the attacker, it can be very difficult to escape when properly applied by an expert. Master these escapes and learn to switch between them quickly as it may be necessary to switch between them as your opponent adjusts to your escape attempts.

1 Pedro's right knee is on Royce's stomach. His left hand holds Royce's left collar and the right hand pulls up on Royce's belt. Royce's left hand grabs Pedro's left wrist.

2 Royce wraps his right arm under Pedro's right leg near the foot and grabs the belt or the back of the pants with his hand. Royce's left hand remains on Pedro's left wrist to prevent him from pulling it.

3 Royce pushes off his feet and first moves the hips in towards Pedro to get further under him. That makes him light and gets his right toes off the ground. Notice that step 3 is very important as the opponent's foot (the one from the knee on the stomach) needs to have the toes off the ground to make him lighter so you are able to force him back.

4 Royce pushes off his feet again and escapes his hips out to his left and away from Pedro. At same time Royce's right hand pulls Pedro's belt down and his left forearm pushes the Pedro's chest back, causing him to fall back. Royce ends up in side control.

Reverse view **A** Notice Royce's grip on Pedro's belt. His arm wraps under the shin and the hand grabs the belt locking the leg in place. **B** Royce first moves his hips in to get under Pedro **C, D & E** and then pulls and pushes in the direction of the trapped foot to force Pedro to fall.

50. Knee on the stomach escape 2

Another great option for escaping the knee on the stomach is shown here by Royce. Both options are equally effective; it is simply a matter of personal preference which one you use. The only difference is in the grip. It may be easier to attain one grip or another depending on the situation, so you should learn to use either escape.

1 Pedro's right knee is on Royce's stomach. His left hand grabs Royce's left collar and the right hand pulls up on Royce's belt. Royce's right hand holds Pedro's pants at the right knee. His left hand grabs Pedro's belt to keep him locked in place.

1 *Detail* Notice how Royce's left hand grabs Pedro's belt right at the center using the stiff arm to keep the distance between him and Pedro's hips. Also check out how Royce's right hand grips Pedro's pants at the right knee, just under the joint and pushing slightly up.

2 Royce pushes off his feet and escapes the hips back and to the left.

3 Royce keeps pushing off his feet and turning until his hips face down. He then pushes Pedro back so he falls. If Pedro resists the fall, Royce will sit back to his left and replace the guard by lifting the right knee in front of Pedro's left leg.

51. Knee on the stomach escape 3

At times your opponent has such a strong grip on you that it is very hard to turn into him. One such grip is when the opponent pulls on your right arm with his left hand and grabs your right leg with his right hand pulling them up and to the left. Rather than fight against Pedro's power Royce again takes advantage of what is given to him and escapes.

1 Pedro has his right knee on Royce's stomach. His left hand grips Royce's right arm while his right hand grabs Royce's right leg with his right hand pulling them up and to the left making it very hard for Royce to turn to his right. Royce tucks his right arm by bending it and bringing the elbow and the forearm close to his body so it is not vulnerable to an arm-lock.

2 Rather than fight Pedro's power Royce takes advantage of his push to the left. He turns to his left and brings the left elbow and forearm under Pedro's right knee and turns slightly back right to create space for his right knee and elbow to come in.

3 Royce brings the right knee up and right elbow down so they touch to create a block under Pedro's right knee. (Notice once again that the use of the knee and elbow together with the forearm and the shin creates an impenetrable barrier.)

4 Royce pushes off his left foot and turns back to the right deflecting Pedro's knee off his stomach and forcing him to the mat. Pedro drops down to the mat.

5 Royce pivots his torso to the left and replaces the guard by bringing his legs in front of Pedro.

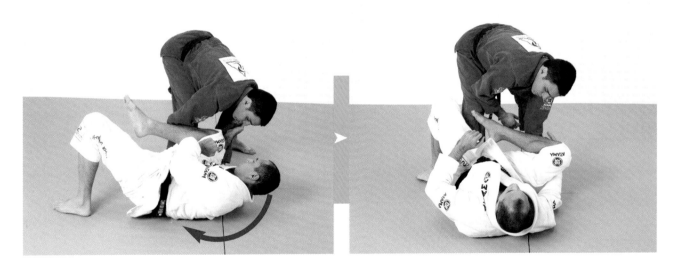

5 *Variation* Should Pedro stand up and step away as Royce removes the knee, he will simply pivot and face Pedro, having his legs in front of him for guard.

HALF GUARD

When it comes to the half-guard Royce believes that less is more. He was brought up in the line of fire in MMA matches and believes that the half-guard is a transitory position in which you are behind on your defense and your opponent is part way to passing your guard.

While many "modern" sports competition fighters have developed their games around the half-guard, Royce believes that is a risky proposition. In the half-guard you are much more exposed to strikes than in the full guard. In light of that Royce believes when you are in the half-guard on the bottom, you should quickly replace the guard, or, if your opponent counters your replace attempt, execute a sweep and reverse the situation to gain a more advantageous position to fight from.

52. Half-guard: Replace the guard or go to back

Royce believes that the key to success in Gracie Jiu-Jitsu is to master and utilize the most efficient techniques for any situation, whether it be a sports match, a submission wrestling match or an NHB fight. For Royce, the half-guard bottom is a position in which you are already late, with your opponent having almost transposed your guard barrier. This may be contrary to the beliefs of some modern sports fighters who think that the half-guard is a practical position to seek and even attack from. When your opponent reaches half-guard your best and most efficient option is to replace the guard and start everything up from a position of advantage to you rather than to him.

1 Pedro reached half-guard on Royce's right side. His right leg is trapped between Royce's legs and his left arm is on the left side of Royce's head. Royce has good defensive posture with his left arm tucked under Pedro's right armpit. Royce's left foot presses on Pedro's right calf to keep it in place.

2 Royce switches and places his right foot on Pedro's right heel, pressing it down to keep it in place. At the same time Royce escapes his hips to his left while turning his shoulders to the right as well.

3 Royce loops the left leg around Pedro's right leg. He hooks the foot on the thigh close to the knee. Royce grabs Pedro's left pants at the knees with his right hand and makes sure his elbow touches the mat.

4 Royce kicks his left leg up using the hook and the right hand to lift Pedro's legs up. He drives him forward and to his left so his head goes towards the mat to the left of Royce's head. Putting Pedro's weight on his head makes Pedro's legs and lower body very light, allowing Royce to move it around easily. From here he can swing Pedro to the left, loop his legs around Pedro's body and replace the guard.

Reverse view Notice how Royce uses his left hook and right hand to drive Pedro up and to his left so his legs are high and his head on the mat. It is a common mistake when executing this technique to lift the opponent square above you. This makes him much heavier and it is much more difficult to accomplish, especially against larger opponents. With his weight resting on his head pressed against the mat Pedro's lower body is light and Royce is able to easily move his legs and replace the guard.

5 *Continuing with the reverse view* Should Pedro put his weight too far forward, Royce can slide to the right and get further under him and go to the back as he shows here.

53. Half-guard: Sweep

When using the previous technique, sometimes your opponent twists his hips as he resists your efforts to replace the guard. In that case you can just switch and use your legs to sweep him. We pick up the technique from the point when Royce has Pedro's legs in the air and the head on the mat on his left side

1 Royce uses his leg and arm to lift Pedro's legs in the air and drop the head on the mat on his left side. Pedro resists the move by twisting his hips as he tries to get back to center.

2 Royce takes advantage of Pedro's over-commitment and loops his right leg around Pedro's left leg. He kicks the heel to the left while at the same time he kicks his left foot to the right to spin Pedro's legs counter-clockwise. At the same time Royce shoots his left arm to the right to force Pedro's chest over, sweeping him.

3 Royce ends up mounted on Pedro.

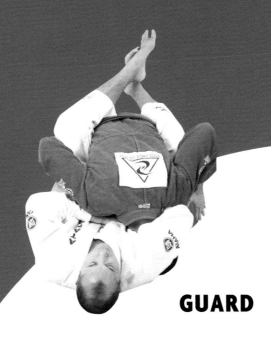

GUARD

The guard is arguably the most important position in Gracie Jiu-Jitsu. Being able to survive and even win with your back on the ground is a huge advantage. While most martial arts teach you to fight from an advantageous position (either standing or being on top), a Gracie Jiu-Jitsu fighter is comfortable even when fighting with his back on the ground.

With your back on the ground and your opponent either between your legs (closed guard) or with your legs between you and your opponent (open guard) the guard is a very complex position. There are so many variations, nuances, techniques and strategies that a whole series of books can be written about it. In this section Royce demonstrates his favorite and most effective techniques from the guard.

As in any other position, Royce believes that when fighting from the guard you must first protect yourself before you strive to attack. This does *not* mean being passive. If you simply defend without countering, you allow your opponent a great advantage and eventually he may succeed in transposing passing the defensive barrier of the guard.

Royce believes that when fighting from the guard you should always try to break down your opponent's posture. Make sure you take advantage of his mistakes, either by countering his moves or by initiating your own attacks. Be alert to the opponent's body position and take advantage of his weight shifts and over-commitments.

GUARD

54. Stand up in base

While Gracie Jiu-Jitsu gives you the tools to survive and even thrive when your back is on the ground, your game is never complete unless you know how to properly stand up in base. The key to properly standing up in base is first to protect yourself from being struck by the opponent and second to effectively use the forward kick to create enough distance to allow you to get up.

1 Royce is on the ground with Pedro standing in front of him ready to strike. Royce has good defensive position: his right leg is forward, the foot planted on the ground and the knee up protect his torso. Royce's right forearm is positioned with the elbow just above the knee to protect his face. Royce's left arm is posted back as a brace. Royce's left leg is cocked and ready to fire a forward thrusting kick.

2 Using his left hand and right foot as base, Royce raises his hips off the ground and extends the left leg to shoot the left foot in a forward thrust kick. The secret to generating power in this kick is the hip swinging forward to create the thrust. Royce's kick is aimed at Pedro's knee which forces him to lean back.

150

3 Royce takes advantage of Pedro's retreat and the push on Pedro's leg to swing the hip back and slide the leg under his hips. He plants the foot back so he has a three-point stance with his feet and left hand. Notice that throughout the movement Royce keeps his eyes on Pedro and the right arm always protects his face.

4 Royce stands up and gains a fighting stance with his fists ready to punch.

55. Rock and kick

Being able to properly defend yourself from an aggressor and keep him at bay is imperative if you are to survive an aggressive attack. The standing up in base technique as shown previously works well once the opponent remains square in front of you, but many times the aggressor will circle around looking for openings to strike you. The "rock and kick" technique allows you to follow your opponent while keeping him at bay until you find the proper time to stand up in base. The key to the rock and kick is connecting your body with the core so you can use the swing of your legs and torso to move your body around.

1 Pedro stands in front of Royce, ready to strike. Royce leans back and coils his legs so his feet block Pedro's strikes. Royce's fists are in front of his face to protect it.

2 As Pedro circles to his left Royce swings his legs up and down using a teeter-totter motion to follow Pedro. When Pedro stops in front of him and sets up a strike with his left leg forward Royce uses his right foot to kick his knee.

3 As he kicks forward Royce can switch to the round-house kick as well. Royce kicks forward striking Pedro's shin and stopping his forward motion. Royce drops the right foot down in front of Pedro's left foot and, pushing off his left hand, swings his left leg for a roundhouse kick to Pedro's face.

56. Pulling guard from the clinch

Although a Gracie Jiu-Jitsu fighter does not necessarily want to be on the bottom with his back on the ground, at times, because of your opponent's size or special ability, that can be a desirable position. Of course you do not want to bring the fight to the ground and then end up in a disadvantageous position, so being able to properly pull guard from a clinch is an important skill.

1 Royce and Pedro are in the over-under clinch.

2 Royce steps on Pedro's right foot with his left foot (forward foot steps on the opponent's forward foot) locking it in place.

3 Royce then steps with his right foot on Pedro's left foot. At this point Pedro cannot walk back or forward.

4 Royce leans slightly back and sits down pulling Pedro's head and arms with his hands. Pedro follows Royce down. When his butt touches the ground Royce wraps his legs around Pedro's waist and locks the feet behind his back, reaching closed guard.

57. Guard attack: Kimura

The kimura is one of the main attacks from the closed guard. Any time your opponent has one or both of his hands on the mat he is open for this attack. Be alert to this situation and take advantage of it. Royce believes that in order for them to work at the highest level, techniques need to be linked together. If one doesn't work you can automatically go to the next one and so forth. The next three techniques are examples of that and are favorites in Royce's arsenal. Use this and other linked sequences that Royce demonstrates to play around with different options and develop your own favorite combinations.

1 Gui is inside Royce's closed guard with has his hands on the ground. Royce's fingers grab Gui's triceps with the palm of the hand blocking the biceps for control.

2 Royce's left hand slides down Gui's right arm and grabs his right wrist to prevent him from pulling it out.

3 Royce opens the legs, plants the feet on the ground and sits up while looping the right arm over Gui's right arm. Royce wraps his arm around until he can grab his left wrist with the right hand.

3 *Detail* Notice Royce's figure-4 around Gui's arm. Royce's right forearm is above Gui's elbow and the forearm touches Gui's forearm. Royce's chest presses against Gui's arm. Royce's right forearm and elbow are on the ground with the left hand locked on to the right wrist.

4 Pushing off his feet, Royce escapes the hips to the left and leans back. His lock on Gui's arm forces it around clockwise. Notice Royce's foot and legwork as he executes the move. His left foot steps over Gui's right leg to lock it in place. Royce's right leg presses on Gui's left side preventing him from stepping over it and moving to his left. Royce ends up on Gui's right side and locks his feet to hold Gui in place and prevent him from rolling over his shoulder to escape the lock. Royce continues torquing Gui's arm in a clockwise direction, almost as if he wanted to touch his right hand on the right ear for the shoulder lock.

4 *Incorrect* If Royce doesn't lock his feet and keep the left leg on Gui's back, Gui can roll forward over his right shoulder and escape the kimura.

58. Guard attack: Guillotine

A very common defense for the kimura from the guard is for the opponent to posture up by dropping his hips down, straightening his back and raising the head up to block your attack. In that case immediately go for the guillotine (second of the three linked techniques).

1 Royce attempts the kimura on Gui's right arm. Gui counters by dropping his hips down, straightening his back and raising the head up. This exposes his neck for the guillotine.

2 Royce wraps the right arm around Gui's neck and slides his hips back. Royce reaches with his left hand and grabs his right wrist. He then tightens the noose around Gui's neck to cinch the choke.

2 *Reverse* Check out Royce's noose around Gui's neck: his left hand grabs the right wrist. The narrow blade of the forearm presses up on Gui's Adam's apple.

2 *Grip detail* Check out Royce's grip and arm position. Royce's forearm points straight up so the narrow blade aims towards the throat. Royce's left hand grabs over the wrist and hand allowing his forearm to press up and in at the same time. The direction of the guillotine pressure is up and in as if he wanted to make a "V" with his forearms.

3 Royce leans back until his back touches the mat. He then pulls the left arm up and extends his legs to apply the guillotine for the submission.

59. Guard: Cross-over sweep

The cross-over sweep is the third part of this sequence from the closed guard. It is most effective when the opponent leans back to counter your kimura and guillotine sequence or when he over-postures by leaning back to avoid the choke. The key to this sweep is to take advantage of the opponent's lean and use your hip to bump him over.

1 Royce has Gui in his guard.

2 Royce sits up and reaches with his right arm to get a kimura on Gui's right arm. Gui counters by straightening his back and raising the head up, exposing it for the guillotine. Royce immediately wraps his right arm around Gui's neck.

3 Gui forces his head back even more to prevent Royce from securing the guillotine wrap.

4 Royce takes advantage of Gui's over-commitment and changes to the cross-over sweep. **A** He lets go of the hold on Gui's head, using the right arm to lasso Gui's right arm instead. **B & C** Royce turns his hips to his left and pushes off his feet to bump the hips up and force Gui to fall over. Notice how Royce's left leg trapped Gui's right leg prior to the bump and prevented him from opening it up to stop the reversal. It is very important for Royce to bump and turn Gui over to the left and not straight back. Also it is very important for Royce to use the pressure of his hips pushing against Gui's chest to turn him over. **D** Royce ends up in the mount.

60. Guard attack: Collar choke

The collar choke is the most basic and important choke from the guard. If you are good at attacking the neck your opponent will have to pay an enormous amount of attention to defend it, opening up a variety of options for you. If he doesn't give the choke the necessary respect it deserves, he will end up having to tap out to the submission or end up unconscious. Here Royce demonstrates another great sequence of linked attacks.

1 Royce has Gui in his closed guard. Royce's right hand grabs Gui's right collar with the standard grip (fingers in and thumb out). Gui has good defensive posture with his right hand blocking Royce's left arm and preventing him from securing the important second grip for the choke. Note: in every choke the second hand is the one that completes the choke, making it final, but the first hand grip is the most important one. Always grip as far back and as deep in the collar as possible with the first hand. This will make even a sloppy second hand grip become effective.

2 Royce circles his left hand under Gui's right arm until it grabs the left collar.

3 Using his legs and arms Royce pulls Gui down and forces his head to the chest. Royce completes the choke by bringing his elbows down towards the mat and close to his side.

3 *Detail* Royce makes sure the narrow blade of his forearm presses on Gui's neck. It is a common mistake to use the wide part of the arm, which makes a much less effective choke.

3 *Incorrect* Another very common mistake for the attacker is to open the elbows for the choking movement. This is much weaker than the proper technique as it relies only on the arm strength for the choke. The proper technique of bringing the elbows down and tight against your sides utilizes the large back muscles to apply the choking pressure, making it much stronger and more effective.

61. Guard attack: Arm wrap lapel choke

A great variation of the lapel choke involves the arm wrap. In the arm wrap the attacker secures full control over one arm by wrapping his own arm around the trapped arm and grabbing the collar with the hand. The arm wrap can lead to many other attacks like arm-bars, key-locks, and omoplatas as Royce demonstrates in the next few techniques. In this first one Royce does the basic arm-wrap lapel choke.

1 Royce has Gui in his closed guard. Gui has good posture. He uses his right hand to grab both Royce's collars at the chest to block him from sitting up. Royce has to break Gui's posture and grip so he grabs Gui's right sleeve with his right hand.

2 Royce circles his left arm under Gui's right arm and at the same times uses the right hand to pull the sleeve and break Gui's grip on the collar.

3 Royce continues to circle the arm around Gui's right arm until he has it completely wrapped. Royce then releases his right hand grip and uses it to open and feed the left collar to his left hand instead. Notice that for most control, Royce's wraps Gui's arm just above the elbow.

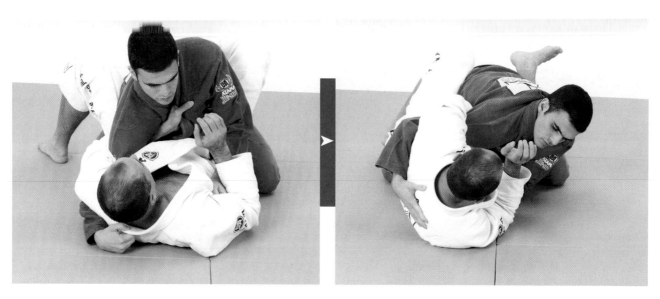

4 Royce opens his legs and pushes off his left foot to escape his hips to the left while bending and locking the right leg at Gui's right hip.

5 Royce grabs the right collar with his right hand. This time he uses the alternative grip: reaching in with thumb inside the collar and fingers gripping the outside. He then locks his feet together to close the guard again. Royce completes the choke by bringing Gui forward with his legs while at the same time he drives the right forearm forward against Gui's throat.

5 *Optional grip* At times the arm wrap is so tight that it may be difficult to grip the inside of the collar with the thumb. In that case Royce grabs the back of Gui's gi at the right shoulder. Royce applies the choke much in the same way – by driving the right forearm against Gui's throat while pulling the left collar with his left hand.

62. Guard Attack:
Arm wrap choke to omoplata

A smart opponent when faced with the arm wrap choke will always try to block the forearm from choking him by pushing the elbow away with his hand. In that case he opens himself for the omoplata shoulder lock. We pick up the attack as Gui blocks Royce's elbow.

1 Royce secures the arm wrap and goes for the choke. He uses his right forearm to press against Gui's throat. Gui counters it by using his left hand to push and block Royce's right elbow to prevent him from applying pressure against his throat with the forearm.

2 Royce opens his legs and pushes off his left foot to escape the hips out. He moves his torso in a clockwise direction until he is approximately 90° from Gui. He then puts his right foot on Gui's left hip and slides his right knee in front of Gui's chest. Notice how Royce's right leg presses up against Gui's chest while the left leg presses down on his back to keep him locked in place.

3 Royce loops the left leg over Gui's right arm and head, locking the arm in as he presses his foot on the ground. The shin pushes on the right side of Gui's face. With the arm secured by the legs Royce can release his left hand's grip on Gui's collar and use both hands to prevent the arm from escaping. Royce slides the left elbow over Gui's right arm and locks the armpit over the wrist. Royce uses his torso movement to bend Gui's arm in an L-shape.

4 Royce continues spinning his body around until he is at 180° in relation to Gui. Royce presses his left leg down forcing the thigh against Gui's right shoulder to prevent him from getting up.

5 Royce pushes off his hands and sits forward. Royce wraps his left arm over Gui's back and grabs Gui's left hip with his left hand. This prevents Gui from rolling over his shoulder and escaping the lock. Royce slides his feet around in a clockwise direction until they are clear under his body.

6 Royce continues to lean forward and slide his legs back. He circles the body around Gui's right arm and uses his hips to force Gui's right wrist forward. He torques the arm around the shoulder joint for the submission.

7 ***Option*** Once he has the omoplata set up Royce can at anytime apply a wrist-lock and submit Gui as he does here. Royce successfully used this in his K1 submission victory over Akebono in 2004 New Years Eve show.

63. Guard attack:
Omoplata escape counters: Toe-hold

Even in the best cases a submission sometimes fails because your opponent anticipates the attack and is quick to apply the proper counter or because you fail to secure all the elements required for it to properly work. In this case Gui escapes Royce's omoplata attack. Royce immediately has this option ready and is quick to apply it.

1 Royce applies the omoplata attack but fails to lock Gui's back with his arm. This lapse allows Gui to roll forward over his right shoulder and escape the submission.

2 Royce intercepts Gui's forward roll and wraps the right arm around Gui's right calf.

3 Royce's left hand grabs the top of Gui's foot. He makes sure his hand is near the toes and the fingers grip the outside of the foot.

4 Royce uses his left hand to grab his right wrist to lock the figure-4 around Gui's right foot. He torques the foot for the toe-hold by pulling the toes down and to his left in a clockwise rotation.

64. Guard attack:
Omoplata escape counter: Biceps cutter

Should he fail to intercept Gui's right leg, or if Gui has very strong legs and Royce cannot control them, he can opt for the biceps cutter.

1 Royce cannot intercept Gui's right leg because Gui forces it down hard, making it difficult for Royce to apply the toe-hold.

2 Royce leaves his left leg bent over Gui's right arm and pulls up on Gui's right sleeve with his left hand.

3 Royce locks his left foot on Gui's right side making sure the blade of his shin points towards Gui's biceps. Royce raises his hips off the ground and starts leaning to his left. Notice how Gui's arm is trapped by Royce's left leg.

4 Royce leans forward with his torso and drops his chest on Gui's chest. He reaches with his right arm under Gui's left arm to prevent him from turning to his right and trying to yank the arm out. Royce then presses his hips down and uses his thigh to press down on Gui's forearm. Royce pushes his shin down on the biceps for the biceps cutter.

4 *Reverse* See how Royce's shin bone presses down on Gui's biceps. Royce's body weight and hips apply the pressure on Gui's arm and biceps for an excruciatingly painful submission.

65. Guard attack: Opponent defends the omoplata: Triangle

Another common omoplata escape has the defender grab his own belt with the hand on the trapped arm to stop the torquing of the arm. The defender then steps out and postures up to force the attacker to roll backwards. In that situation Royce immediately changes to the triangle. Notice that the omoplata is a great transition for the triangle counter as well, so these and the other techniques are linked together.

1 Royce attacks Gui's right arm with the omoplata. Gui is able to grab his belt with the right hand to stop the arm rotation around the shoulder. He steps out with his left foot and pushes off it to raise his torso and bring Royce's legs back, forcing his back to the mat. Royce begins his counter by opening his left leg.

2 Royce rotates his torso to his right and plants his left foot on Gui's right hip. He pushes off the foot to raise his hips up and loops his right leg up and over Gui's left shoulder. He locks the knee over the shoulder. Royce's right hand blocks Gui's left arm to prevent him from reaching Royce's collar to stack him or to block him in case he wants to punch (as in an MMA match).

3 Royce raises his left leg up and locks his right foot under his left calf. At the same time Royce pulls Gui's right arm across his hips until the hand is on Royce's right side. Notice how high Royce's hips are. They are locked right under Gui's right armpit. That is a big key for the success of the triangle. If your hips are low you allow too much space and your opponent can simply yank his arm out.

4 Royce pulls down on his right shin with the left hand to force the leg down on Gui's neck and causing him to lean forward. This allows Royce to adjust his triangle lock and loop the left leg over the right foot for a tighter triangle.

5 Royce further tightens the hold by pulling the right foot with the left hand to lock the left knee over the foot for a very tight triangle on Gui's right arm and head. Royce applies the choke by bringing his knees together and pulling Gui's head down with the left hand. Royce's right leg presses Gui's left side of the throat while Gui's own right arm presses the opposite side for the choke.

66. Guard: Forearm on the throat counter 1 & 2

Although this is not a skilled fighter move, having someone press their forearm on your throat from the guard can cause many to panic and even submit. Worse yet, in a street fight it may cause you to give up your back. The counter to this attack is pretty clever and takes you from a seemingly bad position to a great one, your opponent's back.

1 While inside Royce's guard Gui forces the right forearm on Royce's throat.

2 Gui props up using his bodyweight and the extra boost of driving off his feet to add pressure to the throat. Royce grabs Gui's right wrist with his right hand and the left hand pushes behind the triceps. In one movement Royce extends his body and uses the legs to drive Gui back and release the choking pressure. He drives the arm to the right by pushing the elbow with the left hand and pulling the wrist with the right hand. Without the arm to support the pressure Gui falls forward.

3 Royce wraps his right arm around Gui's head and presses the head against Gui's right triceps to lock the arm in place. Royce grabs the left biceps with his right hand and bends the left arm so his hand presses on the right side of Gui's head for a figure-4. Royce applies the choke pressing his head to the right and squeezing his elbows in.

4 If for some reason he cannot secure the figure-4 for the choke, or as an additional option, Royce can slide to the back. Royce plants the left foot on the ground and pushes off it to slide his hips to the left as he reaches with his left arm around Gui's back until he can control his right wrist.

5 With the wrist controlled by his left hand, Royce starts pulling his body around Gui's until he ends up on his back with hooks on.

67. Guard: Forearm on the throat counter 3: Sweep

At times you may get stuck under your opponent when trying to go to his back. In this case Gui opens his left leg and pushes off it, driving himself to Royce's left and making it difficult for him to slide to the back. Royce takes advantage of Gui's weight commitment and goes for the sweep. Again, these techniques are linked but they are flexible in the order of execution as they are triggered by the opponent's reactions. Generally, the first option is the finish, then taking the back and then the sweep. However, do not make the mistake of getting stuck in that order as it is not set in stone. Instead, remember that Gracie Jiu-Jitsu is about transition and using the techniques that best work for you at any time.

We pick up from the point where Royce grabs Gui's wrist.

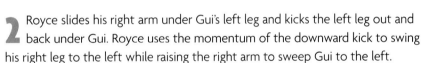

1 Royce deflected Gui's right forearm on the throat to his right and managed to reach around his back and grab Gui's right wrist with his left hand. Gui senses Royce's move and opens the left leg, plants the foot on the mat and pushes off it to drive his body to Royce's left to re-center himself and prevent Royce from going to his back.

2 Royce slides his right arm under Gui's left leg and kicks the left leg out and back under Gui. Royce uses the momentum of the downward kick to swing his right leg to the left while raising the right arm to sweep Gui to the left.

3 Royce ends up side mounted on Gui with his arm trapped.

68. Guard: Arm lock from the guard

Another basic submission from the guard is the arm-lock. Once again do not get turned off by the word "basic" as it means "base", something to build on! From the arm-lock you can transition to a variety of other submissions. When used in conjunction with another basic submission such as the collar choke and its variations, the arm-lock creates a myriad of options that will create havoc in your opponent's mind and destroy his ability to counter as you seamlessly transition from attack to attack.

1 Royce has Gui in his closed guard. Royce's right hand grabs Gui's right collar to set up the collar choke. Gui counters by blocking Royce's left biceps with his right hand to prevent him from getting the second grip necessary for the choke.

2 Royce turns his torso to his right and swings the left arm over the top of Gui's right arm as he tries to reach the left collar. Notice how Gui's right arm is extended as he tries to follow Royce's arm to block it.

3 In one quick motion Royce unlocks his feet, swings the legs back, and shoots the hips up. Royce's left leg goes around and over Gui's head.

4 Royce locks the left calf over Gui's neck and the right calf on his back. Royce grabs Gui's wrist with both hands and drives his heels towards the ground. He pushes off his calves to extend his body and forces the hips up against Gui's right elbow for the submission. The leg swing and finish need to be seamless as you wait for the last moment to control the wrist. Otherwise you will tip your intention and he will pull the arm back early.

69. Guard: Arm lock from the guard: Variation

In this variation Royce uses less of the element of surprise. Instead he controls Gui's right arm from the start. Both options work well – which you use depends on your choice and ability to execute.

1 Royce has Gui in his closed guard. Gui's right hand controls Royce's chest by grabbing the lapels. Royce's right hand grabs the top of Gui's right forearm. Royce locks it in place by bringing his own elbow down and tight against his body.

2 Royce extends the left forearm in front of the left side of Gui's face, using it to block and keep him away. Royce pivots to his right and loops the left leg up and over Gui's head.

3 Royce locks the left calf over Gui's head and the right one over his back. He grabs Gui's wrist with both hands to prevent him from pulling the arm out. Royce presses down and drives his heels to the ground. He extends his body and pushes his hips against Gui's right elbow for the hyper-extension.

70. Guard attack: Arm-lock from the guard: Transition to arm bar

Although you always expect success when you apply a great technique, many times in the development of an attack things can change because, after all, you are fighting against a living and thinking human being. In this case as Royce goes for the arm lock Gui is quick to react and pulls his right arm out. Royce quickly transitions to the arm-bar.

1 Royce applies the arm-lock from the guard.

2 Gui is able to extend his body, open his right leg out and push off it to stack Royce.

3 Gui yanks his right arm out. He escapes the arm-lock but his left arm is extended and vulnerable.

4 Royce turns his head to the right and traps Gui's left wrist between his head and shoulder. He presses his legs down and uses both hands to push down on Gui's left elbow. He curls his torso in for the arm-bar.

71. Guard sequence: Arm-lock from the guard: Transition to omoplata

In the event that Gui's left arm is not extended and Royce cannot trap it for the arm-bar he opts for the omoplata. Again notice how submissions go together: you can insert the omoplata attack variations described previously as you expand your arsenal of attacks.

1 Royce attempts an arm-bar but Gui's arm is not trapped by his head. Royce loops his right arm inside Gui's left arm to force it back.

2 Royce plants the left foot on the ground and pushes off it to turn further to his right. He loops the right leg over Gui's head and grapevines it around his left arm.

3 Royce locks the right foot under his left knee to form a figure-4 around Gui's arm.

4 Royce props off his arms as he sits up. He forces his legs down and presses Gui's left shoulder to the mat. He reaches with his right arm, grabs Gui's right hip, and circles the feet under so his hips force Gui's arm to rotate around the shoulder for the omoplata.

72. Guard: Butterfly or sit-up guard

The "butterfly" or sit-up guard is a great open guard for sweeps and taking the back. The control gained by having the arms wrapped under the opponent's arms make it effective both in sports matches and NHB. Having the feet hooked under the opponent's thighs make it especially effective for submission grappling as not only a way to sweep but as a great way to protect your feet and legs from submission attempts. Royce here demonstrates an effective way to transition from the closed guard to the butterfly.

1 Royce has Gui in his closed guard. His right hand holds Gui's left collar and the right hand controls the right sleeve.

2 Royce pushes Gui's right knee open with his left hand as he opens his legs and plants the right foot on the mat.

3 Pushing off his right foot and left hand, Royce escapes his hips back and to the right. As he turns his body to the left Royce coils his left leg and places the foot on Gui's right hip. Notice that Royce's right hand still controls Gui's left lapel to prevent him from stepping away and disengaging.

4 Royce pushes off the left foot and moves his hips further back to create the space to loop the right leg over Gui's left leg and hook the foot under the thigh.

5 Royce loops his left leg over Gui's right leg and hooks the foot under his thigh. Royce sits up by pulling himself up by the right hand and slips the left arm under Gui's right arm.

6 Royce slips the right arm under Gui's left arm and locks his hands behind his back. Royce's hips are away from Gui's and his head pushes on Gui's chest or shoulder. Notice that these are two keys to the butterfly guard. Your head always needs to be on his chest otherwise your opponent can drive forward and flatten your back to the ground. For the same reason and to help you with sweeps you need distance between your hips and your opponent's hips. If your hips are too close you won't have the proper base and distance to initiate your sweeps.

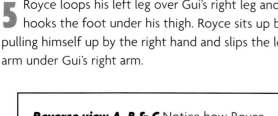

Reverse view A, B & C Notice how Royce pushes off the right foot to move the hips back and to the right so he can lock the left foot on the hip. **D, E & F** Royce sits up and hooks his arms under Gui's arms making sure his head presses on Gui's chest and is below Gui's head.

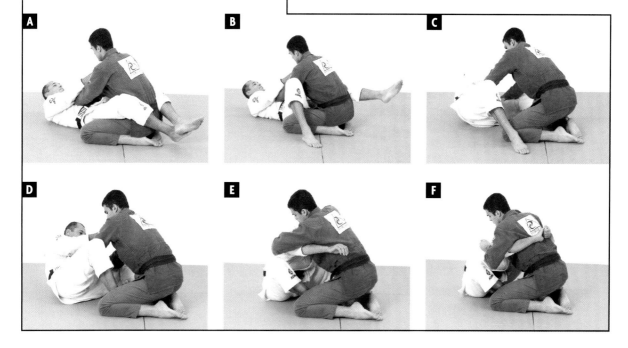

73. Guard: Butterfly guard to hook sweep

Arguably the most common and effective attack from the butterfly guard is the hook sweep. The hook sweep is the beginning of all actions, the movement that sets up most of the options from this guard. Because it is the staple of this guard and because of its apparent simplicity, it is important to understand the mechanics and details of this sweep otherwise you will likely fail and end up either flat on the ground or with your guard passed.

1 Royce has Gui in his butterfly guard. Since his head is on Gui's right shoulder he initiates the sweep to that side.

2 Royce slides the left hand in front of Gui's right arm and loops his left arm around it. He grabs the elbow with his hand to trap the wrist with his armpit. Royce slides his head to the outside of Gui's right shoulder. With his right arm trapped Gui cannot block the sweep to his right.

3 Royce dips his head towards his left shoulder and kicks the right leg up and over causing Gui to fall to that side. It is important for Royce to sweep at a 45° angle and not directly to the side. Note: it is extremely important when executing a butterfly guard sweep not to lean back and pull the opponent over you as you begin to sweep. This leads to having your back on the ground and you will end up flattened. Always sweep to the side – direct your opponent's weight to where he has no base and no ability to brace himself.

4 Royce ends up mounted on Gui.

74. Guard: Butterfly guard to hook sweep: Variation

This is a great variation of the hook sweep from the butterfly guard. Royce actually prefers this one to the standard hook sweep because the push on the knee causes the opponent to completely lose his base in the direction of the sweep, making it much easier to reverse him.

1 Royce has Gui in his butterfly guard. Since his head is on Gui's right shoulder he initiates the sweep to that side.

2 Royce slides the left hand in front of Gui's right arm and loops his left arm around it. He grabs the elbow with his hand and traps the wrist with his armpit. Royce slides his head to the outside of Gui's right shoulder. With his right arm trapped Gui cannot block the sweep to his right.

3 Royce puts his left foot on Gui's right knee and pushes off it to move his hips further away and force Gui to lean forward so his weight is on Royce and not on his knees.

A

B

C

D

4 *A & B* Royce starts to dip his head towards his left shoulder while at the same time he pushes Gui's right knee back with the left foot. This causes Gui to lose his base on that side and fall.
C & D As soon as Gui starts to fall Royce kicks the right leg up using the foot hooked under Gui's left leg to kick that leg up and over to complete the sweep. Royce ends up mounted on Gui.

75. Guard: Butterfly guard hook sweep to taking the back

A common reaction and counter to the butterfly guard sweep is for the opponent to push his weight forward and try to flatten you down. In that case, go to the back.

1 Royce has his hooks on. His head is on Gui's right shoulder as he sets up a sweep to that side. Gui resists raising his hips and driving his weight forward as he tries to push Royce back and flatten him down.

2 Royce raises his left elbow to force Gui's right arm up and slide his head under. The back of Royce's head presses on Gui's right triceps to prevent him from looping the arm in front of Royce's face. Gui is now leaning to his own left and Royce has a clear path to the back.

3 Royce drives his head back. This forces Gui's arm forward while at the same time it slides his body to the left, causing Gui to fall forward and flat. At this point Royce can apply the calf cutter or go to the back. This time he chooses to take the back so he reaches with his left hand and grabs Gui's left hip.

4 Royce pulls himself up and over the back as he loops the left leg over Gui's back and hooks the left heel on Gui's left thigh.

76. Guard: Butterfly guard
sweep to calf cutter

In a variation of the previous counter where the opponent drives his weight forward, Royce goes for the calf-cutter instead. The calf-cutter is the quickest option of the two so look for it first unless you prefer to take the back.

1 Royce has Gui in his butterfly guard and starts to sweep him to his left. Gui counters by raising his hips and driving his weight forward to flatten Royce on the mat.

2 Royce ducks his head under Gui's right arm. Once he clears it Royce makes sure to press it against Gui's triceps to drive him further forward and to prevent him from bringing the arm back in front of Royce's face. At the same time Royce slides the right leg over Gui's right leg. Notice how Royce's left foot keeps Gui's right knee in place.

3 Royce crosses his right foot under his left leg to lock it below the knee. Royce makes sure his shin bone points forward. Royce grabs Gui's right shin with the right hand.

4 Royce pulls Gui's right leg up with both hands forcing the calf against his shin bone for the calf-cutter.

4 **_Front view_** Notice how Royce's shinbone pushes directly onto Gui's calf for the painful submission.

77. Guard: Butterfly guard sweep to foot-lock or heel hook

It is not uncommon for the opponent to open his leg or legs and try to block the butterfly sweep. In that case Royce can immediately go for either the foot-lock or the heel hook.

1 Royce attempts the butterfly sweep to his left but Gui opens the legs out and plants his hands open wide to block the sweep.

2 Royce extends the right leg forward until his knee is past Gui's left leg and then coils and brings his right leg back to drive Gui's leg up.

3 Royce hooks his right leg over Gui's left leg and places his right foot on Gui's left hip as he turns his torso to the left. Royce pushes Gui with his right leg to force him to fall back. Royce places his left foot on Gui's right thigh and pushes it back as he wraps his right arm over the left foot to set up either the foot-lock or the heel-hook.

4 Royce locks the right elbow around Gui's left heel, locks his hands together and pulls the right arm up to torque Gui's heel counterclockwise for the heel-hook submission.

4 ***Detail*** Notice how Royce traps Gui's heel with his right arm. The elbow cradles the heel so when he pulls the arm towards his left he torques the heel for the submission.

5 Alternatively Royce can go for the foot-lock. He wraps the right arm around Gui's left leg. His right hand grabs his left collar so his arm is tight around Gui's left ankle.

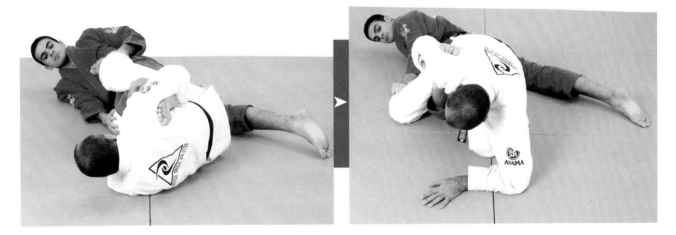

6 Royce rolls over to his left and kneels on top of Gui's left leg. He then leans back to extend the foot with his armpit while driving his hips up for the foot-lock.

78. Guard: Opponent stalls 1: Cervical lock

Many times during a match your opponent will try to stall, especially if he is inside your guard. There are many reasons for that: he may be tired, or time is running out in the match and he is ahead on points. Regardless of his reasons, it is important for you to have a few alternatives to break the stalemate.

1 Gui is inside Royce's closed guard and stalls by pressing his head on Royce's chest while his hands cradle Royce's arms.

2 Royce pushes the top of Gui's head first to the right with his left hand and then, on Gui's resistance, to the right with his left hand. Royce slides his right arm over the right side of Gui's head.

204

3 Royce presses Gui's head to the right with the arm and curls the right leg back over Gui's back so he can grab his right shin with the right hand. Royce locks his feet high on Gui's back.

4 Royce grabs his right leg with both hands and presses his right arm down against Gui's head to force it to the mat.

5 Royce opens his legs, turns his torso to the left and wraps the right arm over Gui's head. He slides the right hand under his left arm at the armpit.

6 Royce locks his hands together. He pulls up on his right arm and drives his elbows in to force Gui's left arm up and the head (locked under his right armpit) down for the cervical lock and the submission.

79. Guard: Opponent stalls 2: Sweep

If his opponent somehow doesn't submit to the cervical hold or in case the lock is illegal (as is the case in many tournaments including the International Brazilian Jiu-Jitsu Federation), Royce applies this sweep instead.

1 Royce underhooks his right arm on Gui's left arm, locks his hands together, and pulls the elbows in to force Gui's left arm back. Royce's right elbow and triceps force Gui's head down. However, instead of applying the pressure on the neck for the cervical hold, Royce opts for the sweep.

2 Royce opens his legs, plants the right foot on the ground and pushes off it to slide the hips to the right.

3 Royce pushes off his right foot and turns his body to his left while at the same time he kicks the left leg in. Once Gui starts falling to the mat Royce kicks the right leg over to add momentum to the sweep.

4 Royce ends up mounted on Gui.

5 Again Royce has the option to apply the cervical hold from this situation should he choose and be allowed to do so. He would apply the pressure by stepping out with the right foot and arching his torso back to force Gui's head in that direction with his armpit.

80. Guard: Opponent stalls 3: Omoplata

In case Royce cannot hook his arm around Gui's head and under the left arm Royce doesn't run out of options. He goes for the omoplata instead. Notice how once again Royce reaches another fork on the road as he gets the omoplata. From here all the omoplata options shown before will work and they can be connected with limitless options. Once you start to understand the connections and how positions are inter-woven and how to transition between them, your game will rise to another level. Keep an open mind and experiment with all of your options.

1 Royce has broken Gui's stall by using his hand to grab the right shin but he cannot hook Gui's right arm with his arm because Gui has his arm tight.

2 Royce braces his right forearm on the right side of Gui's head and slides his hips and torso to the left as he turns to the right. Notice that Royce maintained control over Gui's right arm by dropping his left arm over it and locking the elbow over Gui's elbow.

208

3 Royce circles his torso clockwise so he can loop the left leg over and around Gui's right arm to set up the omoplata.

4 Royce continues circling his body around Gui's right arm. He uses the hips to torque the arm around the shoulder joint for the shoulder lock.

81. Guard: Standing pass defense: Triangle

While some opponents prefer to pass kneeling or crouching low because of the stability and closeness to your hips, others may prefer to pass standing. There are many instances where it is better to stand up and pass (such as if you have a great closed guard) so be prepared to open your guard, defend and attack whether your opponent is standing or not.

Although Royce's next set of techniques are designed against a standing passer, many if not most of them will work – with minor adjustments – when the opponent is passing low with his knees on the ground. One of the great advantages of the standing pass is that you limit the defender's ability to attack your neck with chokes; however there are exceptions, and the triangle is one of them. A common mistake passers make is to leave one arm between the defender's legs without controlling the hips. In that case the triangle is a great option.

1 Gui stands up and tries to use the stacking method to pass Royce's guard. His left hand controls Royce's right leg and his right hand is between Royce's legs pushing down on the chest. Royce's hips are free to move so he goes for the triangle. Royce grabs Gui's right sleeve with the left hand while his right hand holds Gui's left wrist.

2 In one quick burst Royce opens Gui's left arm with the right hand, pushes off his left calf and shoots his hips up while locking the right calf over Gui's neck. Notice that Royce doesn't let go of Gui's right arm — otherwise he will pull it out and foil the attack.

3 Royce pivots the hips slightly to the left and locks the left leg over the right foot to trap Gui's right arm and head in the figure-4 triangle lock. Royce maintains control over Gui's left hand so he cannot grip the collar and try to stack him and pass to the right. Once the triangle is locked Royce will apply the choking pressure by bringing his knees together and pulling Gui's head down with both hands.

82. Guard: Standing pass defense: Triangle opponent hides the arm

A common last resort defense to the triangle has the opponent hiding the trapped arm to prevent the attacker from pressuring it in against the side of the neck for the choke. Here, Gui holds Royce's pants tightly so his right arm pushes out. Royce uses a little trick to achieve the triangle.

1 Royce starts to lock the triangle on Gui. To try to stop the triangle Gui hides his right arm to prevent Royce from fully crossing it in front.

2 Royce grabs the end of his own right pant leg with his left hand and pulls it open so he can reach inside it with his right hand (fingers in and thumb out).

3 Royce tightens up the legs, locks the left knee over the right foot and presses the right forearm into the right side of Gui's neck to complete the choking pressure. To add the most pressure Royce should drive the right elbow down and to the right.

83. Guard: Standing pass defense: Double ankle grab sweep

Everything in life is give and take. While there are many advantages to the standing guard pass there are disadvantages as well. One of those disadvantages is that with your head up and hips high you are less stable than when you are low, leaving you open for sweeps. The most common and highly effective sweep when the opponent is standing is the double ankle grab sweep. The best time to apply this sweep is just as your opponent stands upright but before he is fully set and in base. This sweep works extremely well. Even if you fail on the first try and your opponent somehow regains his balance, go back and persist in it while still holding his ankles and you will succeed.

1 Gui stands as he attempts to pass Royce's open guard. Royce grabs the back of Gui's ankles with his hands to prevent Gui from stepping back. It is important for greatest control that Royce grab the outside of Gui's ankles with all five fingers together to hook the back of the ankle. Royce then drives his heels forward and down towards the ground so the back of his thighs press Gui's thighs in the same direction. Since he cannot step back Gui is forced to fall backwards. This is extremely important; it is a common mistake when applying the double ankle grab to extend the body and shoot the hips straight up. In that case all your power is deflected upwards instead of against the opponent's body.

2 Royce continues driving his heels to the ground until Gui is flat on his back. Royce continues to control Gui's ankles by pulling them up to prevent Gui from sitting back up and fighting Royce's move.

3 Royce pushes off his left hand and sits up to his left. He uses his right arm to pin Gui's chest down and drops the left knee to the ground so he can come over the top over that side and keep his hips low. Royce ends up mounted on Gui. Notice that should Royce go directly to the attempt to mount on Gui, he would have less control and not be as tight. His hips would have to move high which would allow Gui the space to slide one or both knees in front of them and stop his forward progress.

84. Guard: Standing pass defense:
Double ankle grab sweep counter 1: Legs overhead sweep

A very effective counter to the double ankle grab sweep is for the opponent to lean forward. Rather than fight his opponent's counter, this time Royce takes advantage of his momentum forward and goes for the legs overhead sweep. Important: this sweep can be used independently any time your opponent over-commits forward with his weight. A very good key to checking his commitment forward is, anytime you can see your opponent's eyes and head straight above yours it is time to go overhead!

1 Royce attempts the double ankle grab sweep and Gui counters it by leaning forward. Royce releases the ankle grab, using his hands to grab Gui's arms instead.

2 Royce kicks both legs up and over his head to drive them against the back of Gui's arms and force him forward.

3 While still controlling Gui's arms so he can't use them to brace the reversal, Royce turns his head to the left and rolls over his right shoulder. It is extremely important for Royce to select one side to roll over, otherwise both his weight and Gui's weight will press on his neck.

4 Royce completes the movement and ends up mounted on Gui.

85. Guard: Standing pass defense:
Double ankle grab sweep counter 2: Overhead kick sweep

Another common counter to the double ankle grab sweep is for the opponent to drop down and bend the knees. In that case Royce prefers to use the overhead kick sweep. Again this sweep can be used anytime your opponent commits in such manner. Use the same key as in the legs overhead sweep, however your opponent's head does not have to be perfectly above yours but simply near perpendicular.

1 Royce attempts the double ankle grab sweep and Gui counters it by bending his knees and dropping his hips slightly down. Royce releases the ankle grab using his hands to grab Gui's arms instead.

2 Royce pulls himself under Gui with his arms, scooting his hips slightly forward, and plants both feet on Gui's hips.

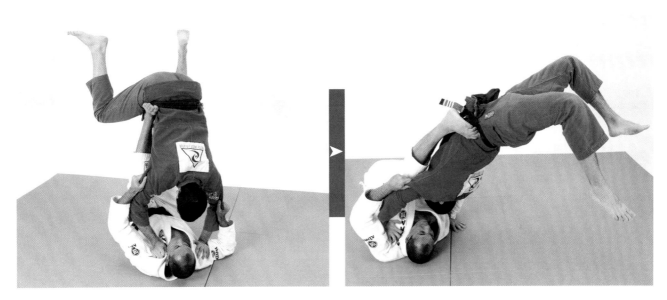

3 Royce extends his legs to push Gui up. He turns his head to the left and rolls over the right shoulder.

4 Royce completes the overhead kick sweep and ends mounted on Gui.

86. Guard: Standing pass defense: Overhead kick sweep variation

Royce presents here a very solid and flashy variation of the overhead kick sweep. Instead of completing the sweep Royce switches to the arm-lock. Both opti~~~~~~~~~~~~~~~~~~~~~~~~~re advanced re~~~~~~~~~~~~~~~~~~~~~~~t off.

1 Royce has Gui in his open guard and Gui leans forward to counter a double ankle grab sweep. Royce puts his feet on Gui's hips while controlling the arms.

2 Royce extends his legs to shoot Gui straight up. Royce wants to attack the right arm.

3 At the height of the flight Royce turns Gui's hips to the right with his feet, extends the right leg and coils the left one slightly.

4 As Gui falls back to the ground Royce loops the left leg over his head and locks the legs for the arm-lock.

5 Gui lands on his back with his right arm extended for the arm-lock

87. Guard: Standing pass defense: Toreana counter

The "toreana" or bullfighter's pass is a favorite passing technique from standing. In this pass the attacker controls the defender's pants with his hands and drives the legs to one side to pass to the opposite side. Royce believes quick reaction is better than late remedies so in this case he breaks Gui's control and replaces his foot position.

1 Gui grabs Royce's pants with the hands. Should Royce fail to react, Gui will toss Royce's legs to one side and step around to the other to reach side control in the toreana pass.

2 Royce grabs Gui's right sleeve with his right hand and circles the left hand around Gui's wrist.

3 In a sudden jerk Royce kicks the left leg out and pulls his arms to the right to bust Gui's grip on his pant legs.

4 Royce keeps the right foot on Gui's left biceps and places the left foot on Gui's right hips. Royce grabs Gui's right sleeve at the elbow with his left hand and pulls the arm down with both hands to replace the guard.

88. Stand-up guard defense:
Toreana counter 2: Open guard sweep

Another great counter to the toreana guard pass is shown here. Again the key to preventing any pass, especially the toreana, is to take away your opponent's control over your legs and/or hips. In this case Royce loops his leg around Gui's arm to regain control. Notice that this sweep does not have to be used only as a counter to the toreana. You can use it anytime you have open guard and can reach the same control with the leg wrapped around the opponent's arm. Also notice how Royce cleverly baits Gui into passing to the preferred side (away from his hook) so Royce can sweep him.

1 Gui stands and tries to pass Royce's guard. He grabs both legs with his hands.

2 Royce needs to break Gui's control over his legs so he reaches up and grabs Gui's right sleeve with his left hand and circles his left leg around that arm until he locks the foot behind the triceps.

3 While still keeping the hold on Gui's right sleeve and the foot hooked around the arm, Royce drops the right leg down to leave a clear path to the right for Gui. He hooks the right foot on Gui's right hips to block him from coming too close. Royce grabs Gui's left leg with the right hand.

4 Gui walks to Royce's right. Royce waits until he reaches the side and tries to put the weight down to stabilize the position.

5 At that exact moment Royce kicks the left leg up and towards his left as he pulls up on the left pants with his right hand to sweep Gui over his own right shoulder to the left.

6 *Side view and reverse* Notice how Royce's shin points down as he drops his hips down and presses against Gui's biceps for the submission.

6 Royce takes advantage of his leg's position, which is still hooked on Gui's right arm; he drops the knee to the ground but leaves the toes on the opposite side so his shin points down on top of Gui's biceps. Royce drops his weight down and presses Gui's forearm against his own arm, which pushes Royce's shin onto the biceps for the biceps cutter.

89. Guard: Standing pass defense: Toreana counter option: Triangle

Many times when you break the opponent's grip and pull the arm down, he will lean forward with his torso, allowing you to slip a triangle on him. Notice that yet again this position works independently of whether Gui is attempting a toreana pass or simply allows Royce to control the arm and place the feet on the hips without fighting to gain posture.

1 We pick up the position as Royce has broken the grip (technique 87, step 4). Royce uses both hands to grip Gui's right arm, the right hand on the wrist and the left on the elbow. Royce's right foot pushes against Gui's left biceps and the left foot pushes on Gui's right hip.

2 In a sudden burst Royce pushes off his left foot and lifts his hips to shoot the right foot up and release the pressure on Gui's biceps while at the same time he pulls the right arm down to force Gui to fall forward. Royce locks the right leg over Gui's head.

3 Royce loops the left leg over the right foot and locks it at the knee for the triangle choke.

90. Guard: Standing pass defense: Tripod sweep

Royce again takes advantage of the weakness of the standing guard pass – instability. When Gui tries to pass and fights for control of the legs Royce quickly switches to the tripod sweep. Royce starts from the same previous open guard control.

1 Royce has the open guard control with the hands grabbing Gui's right arm and the feet placed on the left biceps and the right hip. Gui has his right foot forward.

2 Royce turns to his left side and grabs the back of Gui's right ankle with his left hand. Notice that once again Royce grabs on the outside of the ankle and uses his hands as a hook with all fingers together.

3 Royce drops the right leg down and hooks the foot behind Gui's left knee.

4 Royce extends his left leg and pushes Gui's hips back. Since Gui cannot step back with his legs, which are controlled by Royce's left hand and right foot, he falls back. Royce takes advantage of Gui's momentum to help himself up as he keeps control of the right sleeve and uses it to pull himself up.

5 Royce brings the right foot back and drops the knee over Gui's right leg to trap it between his knee and toes. Royce drives Gui's right arm to his left and forces his back flat on the ground. Royce reaches under Gui's head with his left arm and gets in side-control.

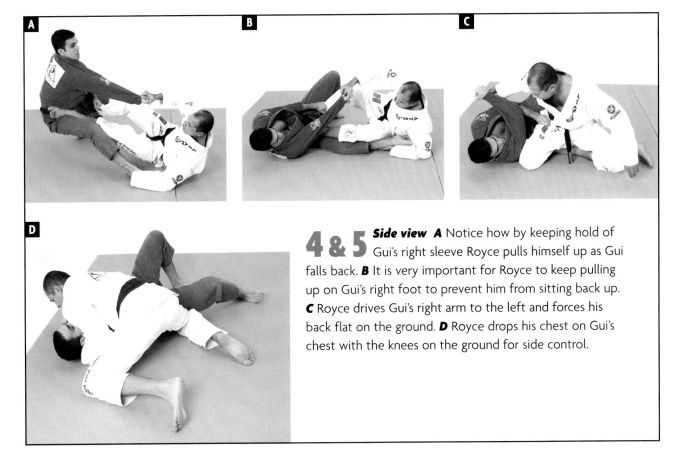

4 & 5 **Side view** **A** Notice how by keeping hold of Gui's right sleeve Royce pulls himself up as Gui falls back. **B** It is very important for Royce to keep pulling up on Gui's right foot to prevent him from sitting back up. **C** Royce drives Gui's right arm to the left and forces his back flat on the ground. **D** Royce drops his chest on Gui's chest with the knees on the ground for side control.

91. Guard: Standing pass defense:
Tripod sweep counter 1: Foot-lock

A cagey advanced opponent will know how to counter the tripod sweep by driving his near hip forward and the knee points in to take away your angle and deflect the power of your leg's push on his hip. Of course for him to be successful countering it he has to react quickly and precisely. In the event that he successfully counters, Royce has a great transition ready and goes for the foot-lock.

1 Starting from the previous open guard control, Royce goes for the tripod sweep by grabbing Gui's right ankle with his left hand but Gui reacts by driving the right hip forward and pointing the knee in.

2 Royce kicks the left leg forward, under and around Gui's right leg until his left foot locks on Gui's right hip. Royce slides his left hand down to Gui's right heel and pulls it open (counter-clockwise direction) to force the leg to buckle in more.

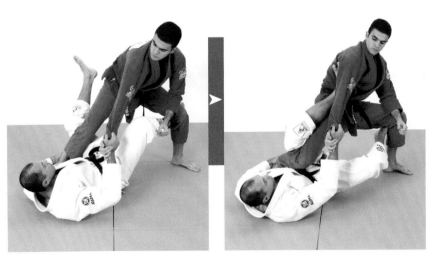

2 **Option** Royce can hook the right foot behind Gui's left knee as he loops his left leg around Gui's right leg and sweep Gui backwards instead of forward by kicking the right foot forward as he extends the left leg.

3 Royce continues pulling Gui's right heel and drops his right foot to Gui's left leg just below the knee. Royce extends his legs to push Gui away and force him to fall. Royce slides his left elbow over Gui's right heel to lock the leg between his arm and leg and trap the foot under his armpit.

4 Royce continues turning to his right until his stomach faces down and wraps the left arm around Gui's right ankle. Royce grabs his right collar with his left hand and applies the foot-lock by arching his torso back to extend Gui's foot backwards with his armpit.

92. Guard: Standing pass defense: Tripod sweep counter 2: Sickle sweep

Royce here presents another option from the tripod counter when the opponent drives his hip forward, the sickle sweep. Again Royce takes advantage of whatever his opponent gives him and goes for the best available option. In this case, since Gui turns his hip in, he doesn't have balance on his back leg and Royce exploits the weakness.

1 Royce switches from the open guard to the tripod sweep. As he grabs Gui's ankle, Gui counters by driving his right hip and knee in to deflect Royce's power.

2 Royce immediately changes to the sickle sweep. He turns further to his left side and drops the left leg down to the ground so the heel is just back of Gui's left ankle.

3 Royce kicks the left leg back in a sickle like motion and cuts Gui's left foot off the mat to take away his base. At the same time Royce pushes with his right leg on Gui's left hip and maintains his control over the right ankle with his left hand to force Gui to fall backwards.

4 Royce holds onto Gui's right sleeve with his right hand and uses Gui's falling momentum to help pull himself up. Royce drops the right knee over Gui's right thigh while still keeping the toes on the mat to trap the leg and prevent Gui from trying to replace the guard. Royce drives Gui's right arm to his left to force his back flat on the ground.

5 Royce reaches under Gui's neck with his left arm, slides the left leg forward first and turns his hips down. Only *after* he clears the left leg will Royce step over with the right one, otherwise Gui can use his legs to trap Royce's left leg into half-guard.

93. Guard: Standing pass defense:
Take the back

Another clever option from the open guard is taking the back. Royce really likes this attack as he likes any opportunity to control the opponent's back. Again all options are somewhat interchangeable and your choice will depend on personal preference and the opponent's reactions. In this case Royce helps achieve the proper reaction by pushing forward with his legs to cause Gui to push back against them.

1 Royce has open guard on Gui. He dominates the right arm with both hands and uses his right foot to push against Gui's left biceps and the left foot to push against the right hip. To set up the move Royce pushes forward with his legs. Gui reacts and pushes back.

2 On Gui's reaction Royce releases the left foot from Gui's hip and pulls the right arm across his body, while at the same time he pushes off his right leg to escape the hips to the left, causing Gui to fall forward. Notice how Royce extends his arms to push Gui's right arm — this both takes away his balance and prevents him from reaching back and grabbing the gi to re-center himself and block the path to his back.

3 Royce ends up on Gui's right side with a clear path to his back. Royce continues pushing Gui's right sleeve forward with his right hand and reaches around the back with his left until he grabs either the collar or just under the armpit.

4 Royce pulls himself over Gui's back and locks the left heel on his hip for the second hook.

2, 3 & 4 *Front view* Notice how Royce uses his left foot and arms to help escape his body to the left so he can reach over and grab Gui's armpit and pull himself to the back. Remember Royce's right leg was in front of Gui's right leg so the heel hooks automatically in front of his right hips. Also notice how Royce keeps his right arm straight to force Gui's right arm forward so he cannot reach back and grab Royce's gi and pull him back.

94. Guard: Standing pass defense: Push and trip

This sweep is very clever, very simple and very effective. When it works it is somewhat demoralizing to the opponent. The key to the push and trip is timing and the element of surprise. Don't try using this sweep too often, otherwise your opponents will catch on and easily avoid it. However, in the heat of the battle if your opponent takes a moment to stop and rest to reassess the situation, that is the best time to use it.

1 Gui is attempting to pass Royce's guard. At this point he is not grabbing onto anything (the sweep won't work if he is grabbing your gi). Royce has his feet on Gui's thighs to keep distance.

2 In one quick motion, Royce sits up, places his feet behind Gui's ankles to block them from stepping back and pushes Gui's chest with both hands to make him fall back. Notice how Royce curls his toes back to lock Gui's ankles in place. Also notice how his left leg lifts Gui's right leg up to prevent him from easily sitting forward.

3 With Gui on the ground Royce scoots his hips forward, places his right shin between Gui's legs in front of his hips and kicks the left leg under Gui's right leg. Royce wraps the left arm around Gui's right ankle and traps the foot with his armpit and grabs his own right collar with the left hand.

4 Royce locks his left foot on Gui's right hip. He closes his knees together to trap Gui's right leg and arches his torso back to apply the foot-lock on Gui's right foot. Royce's pressure comes from leaning back. His armpit drives Gui's toes back while at the same time he raises his hips up to force them against his forearm. Royce pushes the blade of the forearm against Gui's right Achilles for the submission.

95. Guard: Low passing defense: Loop choke

Defending the guard involves many elements, including guard replacement, sweeps and, best of all, counter-attacks. One cannot expect to succeed with only one option all the time, so learn and practice a variety of aspects of the defense, especially the submissions. One of Royce's favorite submissions when the opponent is passing low is the loop choke. This is a sneaky choke as the opponent believes he is succeeding in his quest to pass until it is too late to defend himself.

1 Gui attempts to pass Royce's guard. His hands are busy controlling and pinning Royce's legs. Royce has his right elbow propped on the ground and leans to his right, almost giving a clear path for Gui to pass and reach side control, but there is a catch: Royce's left hand grabs Gui's left collar (standard grip). Since this choke relies on a feint Royce does not want to call too much attention to the collar so he grabs it lightly and low. If he were to grab high and tight against Gui's neck or pull on it, it would alert Gui to the impending danger.

2 Gui continues to move to his right to pass the guard. Royce sits up and loops the left collar under Gui's neck while at the same time he pulls Gui's head down with the right hand to direct the head under the left arm.

3 Royce drops his torso to the right as he lifts the left elbow over Gui's head to fully complete the loop around the neck. Royce gets his back flat on the ground and with his right hand grabs Gui's right arm to prevent him from rolling clockwise and releasing the loop.

3 **Detail** See how Royce's left hand pulls Gui's collar around his neck. Also notice how Royce's right hand grabs Gui's right arm to prevent him from rolling to his left and escaping the choke.

4 Royce continues circling under Gui's torso (counterclockwise direction) so his head is under Gui's chest and applying pressure on the loop choke. Royce pushes off his right leg and continues applying pressure with the loop to choke Gui. Gui's last resort effort tries to loop his left leg over to release pressure.

5 Royce follows his rotation and ends up on the north-south position with his chest pressing down on Gui's chest and the loop choke fully tightened for the submission.

96. Guard: Low passing defense:
Double underhooks counter: Shoulder lock

The double underhooks pass is a very safe and effective passing technique. It is a favorite against defenders who have good triangles and arm-locks because the arms are hooked *under* the legs. The best bet to defend against this pass is to prevent the attacker from gripping your belt and controlling your hips, but this counter will work even in the event he is successful at controlling your midsection.

1 Gui is trying to pass Royce's guard. Royce is in the butterfly guard.

2 Gui switches to the double underhooks method. He locks both arms under Royce's legs and will try to pull him forward while throwing his legs back to stack him. Royce grabs Gui's wrists with his hands to keep him from pulling them away.

3 Royce decides to attack the right shoulder, so he pushes off his right hand, slides his torso to the left and passes the left foot in front of Gui's hips until he can lock it on the outside of Gui's left hip.

4 Royce extends the left leg while bringing the knee in to center. This applies downward pressure on Gui's triceps for the shoulder lock on Gui's right shoulder.

3 & 4 *Side view* Notice how Royce locks the left foot on the outside of Gui's left hip while still holding the right wrist with his left hand. When Royce extends his leg and turns his knee in, he applies pressure to Gui's right shoulder in an action somewhat like a key-lock.

97. Guard: Low passing defense: Sweep

Often your opponent will grab your belt with both hands and push away as a way to break your closed guard open. This is a very powerful grip and a solid way to achieve that goal. If you don't react your guard will be opened and you will be at a disadvantage on the timing. Royce likes to get ahead and always have a strong option to take advantage of any situation—here, he goes for a sweep.

1 Gui is inside Royce's closed guard and wants to break it open and pass low. He grabs Royce's belt with both hands and extends his arms to gain posture and to push away and break the guard. Royce grabs Gui's left sleeve with his left hand and circles the right arm under the left arm.

2 Royce turns his torso to the left as he pulls Gui's left sleeve to the left and drives the right arm up to break Gui's grip on the belt.

3 Royce pulls Gui's arm across his body, props off his left elbow and sits up as he grabs Gui's right armpit with his right hand. Royce opens his legs, plants the right foot on the ground and escapes the hips to the right. Gui raises his torso to protect his back.

4 Royce opens the legs wide. He swings the left leg towards the right and scissors the right leg in while he drops off his left elbow to generate momentum and sweep Gui to the right.

98. Guard: Low passing defense: Take the back

At times when faced with the previous attack, the opponent will drop his torso down and drive his weight to the right to foil the sweep attempt. No problem! Royce doesn't like to fight with the opponent and instead takes advantage of his commitment to the right to take the back around his left side. Notice that this and the previous position are perfectly interchangeable, depending on the opponent's reaction. If he stays with his torso high, the sweep is the best option, if he drops his torso and pushes his weight to the right, take his back! We pick up the position from the point where Royce has already broken Gui's grip and pushed the arm across.

1 Royce pulls Gui's left arm across his body and grabs the right armpit with his right hand as he opens his legs, plants the right foot on the ground and escapes the hips to the right. Gui drops his torso and leans to his right to block the sweep.

2 Royce opens the legs and starts pulling himself around Gui to take the back.

3 Royce continues his path around Gui's back and hooks his left leg on Gui's left leg.

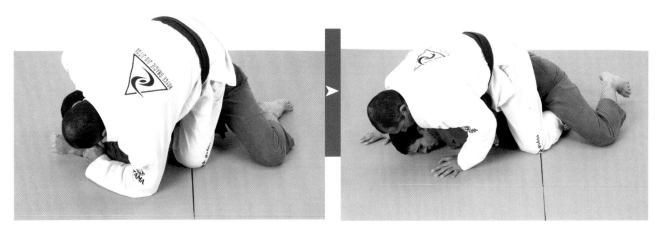

4 Royce continues circling around Gui's back. Notice that up to this point Royce still has control over Gui's left arm and drives it forward. Otherwise Gui could swing the arm back in front of Royce's head and grab the grip to block his motion. Royce only releases Gui's left arm grip *after* he locks the right leg in front of Gui's right leg for the second hook. He has now completely taken back control.

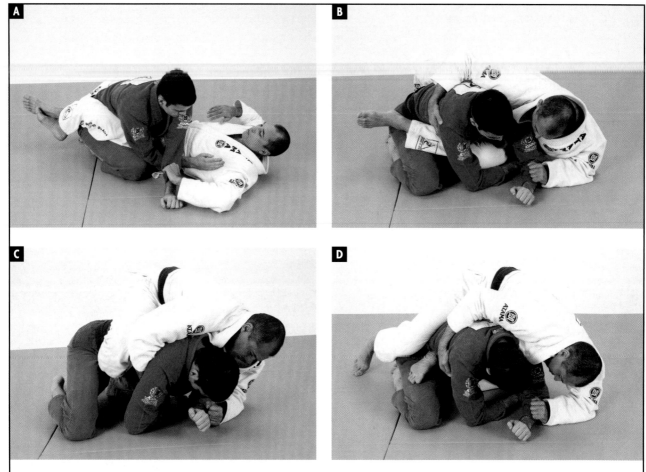

Reverse view: **A & B** Royce keeps pushing Gui's arm and grabs the right armpit with his right hand. **C & D** Royce continues his path around Gui's back and locks the right leg in front of his right leg for the second hook.

5 **Option** Should Gui once again raise his torso to fight Royce and take his back, Royce can quickly switch to the arm-lock. He arches his torso back to extend Gui's left arm and places the right forearm in front of Gui's face to keep the distance. Royce swings the right leg over the head and turns stomach down to press his hips against Gui's elbow to hyper-extend it.

99. Guard: Low passing defense: Step over sweep

Another common passing technique is to step over the defender's legs and gain side control. This pass relies on control of the legs and a slow stepping process to trap the legs with your legs until you reach your objective. Royce first tries to block the path with his knees, but should the attacker insist on forcing the pass he has a perfect and unusual sweep that ends up in a foot-lock for that situation.

1 Gui is inside Royce's closed guard with the right hand on the belt. He steps back with the left leg, turns his torso left and uses the left hand to push down on Royce's right leg to pass to Royce's right.

2 Royce plants the left foot on the mat and pushes off it to escape the hips to the left. He places the right foot on Gui's left thigh and slides the left knee in front of his hips to block his path.

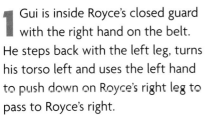

3 Gui drops the left knee over Royce's right thigh and continues forcing the pass.

4 Gui continues to pass to his own left. Instead of trapping Gui's right leg with his legs and securing the half-guard, Royce slides the left arm under Gui's left armpit and uses his hands to push on Gui's left side. Royce brings the right heel towards Gui's right leg to lock that leg between his right calf and left shin. Notice that Royce's left shin is pushing against Gui's hips.

5 Royce drives Gui away by extending his left leg and pushing with the left hand against the left side of Gui's ribcage. He pivots his torso to his right (counter-clockwise). Royce locks the left elbow over Gui's left leg.

6 Royce pivots around Gui's left leg and drops the right knee to the mat. He brings the right elbow to touch the right thigh to keep Gui's ankle trapped. When both his knees are on the mat Royce raises his torso and lassoes the right arm around Gui's left ankle. He then grabs his own left collar with the right hand. Royce applies the foot-lock by arching his torso back so his armpit pushes Gui's toes back and his forearm pressures Gui's Achilles.

100. Guard defense: Scissors sweep

The scissors sweep is one of the staple sweeps from the guard. Although it is one of the most basic sweeps, and one of the first sweeps you ever learn from the guard, it is extremely effective when properly used. It is especially effective in combination with a choke or when using different variations of the grip to counter-sweep or take the back, as Royce will show here in the next few techniques. There are several keys to an effective scissors sweep and we will point them out as the technique develops.

1 Gui steps back with the left leg and gains posture as he attempts to pass Royce's guard. His right hand controls Royce's collars to maintain his base and distance and his left hand controls Royce's belt to prevent the hips from moving up. Royce's right hand grabs inside Gui's right collar and the left hand grabs the right sleeve near the elbow.

2 Royce unlocks his feet and presses down on Gui's left thigh with his right calf. This allows him to turn to his left and pivot his hips away and to the right.

3 Royce brings the right knee and shin in front of Gui's hips until his right foot locks on the outside of the left hip. At the same time Royce slides the bent left leg down to the mat so his heel touches Gui's right knee. *Keys:* Royce needs to have distance between his hips and Gui's, otherwise his right leg will be compressed and he will not have any spring on it. Royce's left heel at the Achilles needs to be on the mat as close to Gui's knee as possible and not up pushing against the thigh, otherwise he has much less leverage for the sweep.

4 Royce pulls Gui's torso up towards his head causing him to lean forward and rest his weight on Royce's right shin. At once Royce scissors the legs, kicking the right leg forward to push Gui's hips to the left and bringing the left back to remove the right knee from the ground and take away his base. This sweeps Gui counterclockwise towards Royce's left side. Royce ends up mounted on Gui. Notice the key here is to pull Gui up towards the head while keeping the right leg stiff, otherwise his weight shift will simply cause your right leg to collapse onto itself and take away the power for the kick.

101. Scissors sweep opponent resists: Counter sweep

Most opponents are familiar with the scissors sweep and will try countering one way or another. One of the most common counters is for the defender to drop his chest and lean away from the direction of the sweep. Royce takes advantage of the change in the weight distribution and sweeps to that direction instead.

1 Royce prepares the scissors sweep to his left by turning to that side so he has his legs in perfect position to scissor Gui. Gui counters by dropping his chest and hips back and leaning to Royce's right.

2 Royce reaches under his right arm and grabs Gui's left sleeve with his left hand to pull the arm across his body. Royce props off his left elbow and reaches over Gui's back and grabs the gi near the right shoulder with his right hand. Notice that at this point Royce could also opt to take Gui's back as he has a clear path to it.

2 *Reverse* Check out how Royce turns more to his left and how the outside of Royce's right leg pushes against Gui's chest.

3 Royce pushes off his left leg and drops his head and torso back. At the same time he opens the right leg out and pulls Gui's right shoulder with the right hand to twist Gui's body in a clockwise direction. This sweeps Gui to the right. Royce ends up in side control on Gui's left side. Royce pushes off his left foot to keep pressure on Gui.

3 *Reverse view* Royce gets a lot of momentum by dropping his back and head to the ground as he pivots to his right. At the same time Royce's right leg opens and drives against Gui's chest. It is important for Royce to continue pulling Gui's left arm across with his left hand as this will help twist Gui in a clockwise direction and assist the sweep.

4 Royce switches the hips by sliding the right leg under the left. He squares his chest with Gui's chest to finish in the classic side control position.

102. Thrusting choke defense

The thrusting choke is a very effective attack when you are inside the opponent's guard. It either surprises, causing panic and leading to a quick submission, or it forces the defender to open the guard. It is very important to be aware of the choke and know how to properly defend it. Royce here not only shows the proper defense but goes one step further and demonstrates a way to prevent the opponent from switching to the other side and repeating the choke again.

1 Gui is inside Royce's closed guard and goes for the thrusting choke. His right hand grabs Royce's left collar with the fingers in and the thumb out. He leans forward to push the hand down against Royce's throat. Gui's left hand pulls down on Royce's right collar to tighten the choke.

2 Royce opens his legs, places both feet on the mat and pushes off them to bridge to his right (same direction of the choking pressure – also same direction as Gui's top hand). The bridge will temporarily relieve the intense choking pressure. At the same time Royce cups both hands over Gui's right hand and brings the elbows together to pull the hand down and further release the choke.

3 Having released the choking pressure Royce drops his hips down and turns to his right. He brings the left knee under Gui's right arm and presses it against his chest.

4 Royce pushes the knee against Gui's chest to create distance and a barrier so Gui cannot lean forward to reapply the choking pressure. At the same time Royce pulls Gui's right hand out and completely defuses the attack.

103. Guard pass:
Double leg grab defense

Another favorite passing technique is the double leg grab. In it the attacker wraps his arms around your knees and pushes the legs together to remove the barrier they form so he can reach side control. This is a very effective passing technique that needs to be properly dealt with. Royce here demonstrates his favorite counter to foil this pass.

1 Gui is able to wrap his arms around Royce's legs and push them together as he tries to pass. Royce immediately props off his right elbow and brings his back off the ground so he has some mobility. If he were to remain flat with his back on the ground Gui could easily walk over and around his legs and reach side control.

2 Gui opens his legs and begins to pass towards Royce's right.

3 Royce places both hands on the right side of Gui's head and extends his arm to push the head away and block Gui's progress. Notice that Royce needs to push the head in the same direction of Gui's passing.

3 *Incorrect* If Royce pushes the left side of Gui's head (opposite direction to Gui's passing) he is actually helping the pass as he forces Gui to pivot *around* his block.

4 Royce turns to his right and continues pushing Gui's head back until he frees one of his knees, in this case the bottom one.

5 Royce pushes off his right knee and drives his body back, breaking Gui's grip on his legs, and returns to center. Royce brings both knees in front of Gui. He hooks his feet under Gui's arm to replace the guard.

104. Guard: Foot-lock defense 1

One of the biggest disadvantages of the open guard is that you are always exposing your feet to foot-locks, especially in controls as in technique 88. There, when Royce actually loops the foot around Gui's arm, he half-way gives the foot-lock hold. When using the open guard, it is important for you not only to be aware of the danger, so you can quickly react, but you also need to know the proper foot-lock defense.

1 Gui stands up in Royce's open guard. Royce controls Gui's right collar with his right hand and the left sleeve with his left hand, Gui sets up the foot-lock by bringing his right leg in and touching his elbow to his thigh to trap Royce's left leg.

2 Gui steps back with his right leg and drives his left knee between Royce's legs. He wraps his right arm around Royce's left ankle at the Achilles and holds his left wrist with the right hand to lock the figure-4 around Royce's foot. Royce immediately senses the foot-lock coming and prepares his counter as he begins to sit up.

3 Gui drops to the mat. He turns his body towards the side of the leg that he attacked to make Royce's escape more difficult. Gui wraps the right leg around Royce's left leg and places his foot on Royce's left hip to push and pin him back. Since his left leg is being attacked Royce props forward off his left elbow and turns to his left.

4 To defend his foot Royce needs to prevent Gui from arching back and extending his foot. The first thing Royce wants to do is shoot his left leg forward so his foot and ankle slide past Gui's noose. This is commonly called "stepping in the boot" as the maneuver mimics that movement. Royce grabs Gui's left leg and pulls himself up to help "step in". At the same time, he pushes Gui's right ankle down with the left hand to remove the block on his hip.

5 Having removed the block on his hip Royce scoots his buttocks to his left and sits on Gui's right ankle to stop him from replacing it in front of his hip.

6 Royce continues sliding his body to his left and forward, making sure to keep his weight on Gui's right leg, otherwise Gui will coil it back and replace the block with the right foot. Notice that Royce never stops pulling himself up by his right hand to stay close to Gui and defend his foot.

7 Royce continues sliding his hips to the left and moving forward towards Gui. Royce grabs Gui's right collar with the right hand and pulls himself even closer to Gui while he swings the right leg around Gui's left leg and drives the right knee forward between Gui's legs. Royce pulls himself completely over the top of Gui and ends up mounted on him.

105. Guard foot-lock defense 2: Opponent closes his legs tight

In this case Gui goes one step further as he drops to the foot lock and locks his knees together to press against Royce's left leg and make it more difficult to use the previous escape. Royce uses this variation instead.

1 Gui attacks Royce's left foot with a foot-lock. He brings his knees together while turning towards Royce's leg to make it very difficult for Royce to escape with the previous technique because Gui's left shin blocks Royce's forward path. Royce props off his left arm and sits forward as he "steps in the boot".

2 Royce grabs Gui's left knee with his right hand and pushes off his left hand to swing himself and Gui to the right side as he grabs Gui's left collar with his left hand.

3 *Reversing the side for better viewing* Royce ends up on his own right side. His left hand pulls up on Gui's collar to allow him to further push his left foot forward and release the pressure. Notice that Gui still has his legs tight to block Royce's forward path.

4 While still pulling on Gui's collar Royce steps back with his right leg and props his right arm back.

5 Royce pushes off his arm and stands, stepping back with the right leg. Notice that Royce keeps pulling on Gui's collar during the entire move as he needs to keep Gui from arching back and releasing the pressure on his foot.

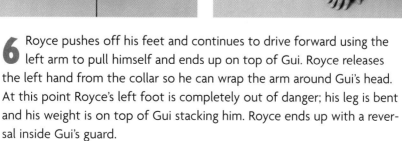

6 Royce pushes off his feet and continues to drive forward using the left arm to pull himself and ends up on top of Gui. Royce releases the left hand from the collar so he can wrap the arm around Gui's head. At this point Royce's left foot is completely out of danger; his leg is bent and his weight is on top of Gui stacking him. Royce ends up with a reversal inside Gui's guard.

106. Guard foot-lock defense 3: Heel-hook

Although he is very patient and prefers to methodically advance on solid grounds than to risk everything for a win, Royce is not against going for the kill when the proper moment arises. In many instances when attacking with the foot-lock, the opponent's foot is vulnerable to the heel hook so look for the opportunity and take advantage of the opening. Note: The heel hook is illegal in some sports tournaments so make sure of the rules before going for this option. This is a perfect option for a street fight or a NHB fight.

1 Gui stands up in Royce's open guard. Royce controls Gui's right collar with his right hand and the left sleeve with his left hand, Gui sets up the foot-lock by bringing his right leg in and touching his elbow to his thigh to trap Royce's left leg.

2 Gui steps back with his right leg and drives his left knee between Royce's legs. He wraps his right arm around Royce's left ankle at the Achilles and holds his left wrist with the right hand to lock the figure-4 around Royce's foot. Royce immediately senses the foot-lock coming and prepares his counter as he begins to sit up.

3 Gui drops to the mat and turns his body towards the side of the leg that he attacked, making Royce's escape more difficult. Gui wraps the right leg around Royce's left leg and places his foot on Royce's left hip to push and pin him back. Since his left leg is being attacked Royce props forward off his left elbow and turns to his left.

4 Royce cups his hands on Gui's left heel and pulls it up for the heel hook.

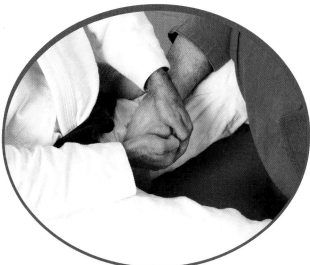

4 **Detail** Notice how Gui's toes are trapped by Royce's crotch and Royce's hands grabbing each side of the heel. Royce pulls the heel towards himself, torquing the heel and the knee to apply the heel hook

107. Guard defense from punches: NHB

Although he is an excellent sports fighter, Royce's fame came not from his sports achievements but rather from real fighting situations in professional events. Royce's claim to fame, especially in the early stages of his career, was his ability to defend himself and even win from a seemingly bad position: being on his back. In the next few techniques Royce will show his secrets of protecting yourself from strikes when you are on your back with the opponent in your guard.

1 Gui is inside Royce's closed guard and wants to punch. Royce wraps his arms inside Gui's arms. He holds the triceps with the hands and uses the forearms to block Gui's arms from punching. Royce needs to control Gui's triceps, otherwise he can swing the arms back again and punch.

2 Continuing with his defense, Royce coils the legs in and puts his feet on Gui's hips. Royce keeps his knees up and in front of Gui's chest. He then opens the knees so the shins push against the biceps to block them. From this defensive position Royce has complete control over Gui. Even as he struggles to free his arms and punch Royce easily follows and controls him.

3 Royce goes for the attack. He kicks the left leg forward and slides the hips to the left while wrapping the left arm around Gui's right arm and trapping the forerm with his armpit.

4 Royce steps down with the left foot and pushes off it to escape his hips back and to the left, causing Gui to lean forward. Notice that Royce kept control over Gui's left arm with his right shin on the biceps and the left hand on the triceps.

5 Royce locks the left leg over Gui's back and presses it down to keep Gui from standing up. He applies a reverse arm-bar by pressing down on the right elbow with his left thigh and arm. Alternatively, Royce can punch Gui's face with his left arm. Notice that Royce controls Gui's left wrist with his right hand to prevent him from gaining any grip.

6 If Gui's wrist escapes from the armpit Royce will transition to a reverse key-lock or kimura instead. Royce grabs Gui's right wrist with his left hand and pushes it back to force the arm to bend at the elbow around his thigh.

7 Royce reaches around Gui's right arm with the right arm and locks the right hand onto his left wrist to secure the figure-4 lock on that arm. Royce pivots his torso to the left and cranks Gui's right arm around the shoulder for the kimura. Notice how Royce presses his knees together to trap Gui.

8 Should Royce miss grabbing Gui's right wrist and Gui be quick to bend and "hide" the arm, Royce can transition to the omoplata. He loops the left leg around Gui's right arm, sits and spins his body clockwise to force the arm around the shoulder for the shoulder lock.

108. Guard defense from punches: NHB Opponent leans back

Sometimes your opponent is able to get away from you and you cannot get control of him right away. Here Gui is able to gain posture, lean back and cock his arms to punch.

1 Gui is inside Royce's closed guard and is able to get back, gain posture and coil his right arm to punch. Royce places his arms, bent at the elbow, in front of his face to block the punches.

2 Taking advantage of Gui's shifting his weight forward to punch, Royce pulls Gui close to him with his legs and wraps the arms over Gui's arms. Notice how Royce sits up with the forearms in front of his face to protect it as he pulls Gui with the legs.

3 Gui falls forward on Royce. In this case Gui's head ends up on the right side of Royce's head.

4 Royce re-locks his legs high on Gui's back. His right arm wraps around Gui's head to prevent him from pulling away and the left hand blocks the right side of Gui's head from head-butting Royce's face. Royce's right arm is in front of Gui's left arm to block it from punching. His left arm blocks Gui's right arm from doing the same. Also since Gui's head and torso are down and close to Royce he cannot get the proper distance to deliver any punches.

4 ***Option*** Royce pushes Gui's face to the right with his left hand and grabs his right shin with both hands. Royce's right arm presses down on Gui's head and forces it down. This not only blocks the head-butts but also the left punches. Royce's left arm is in front of Gui's right arm to block it as well.

5 Royce slightly releases his right arm grip on Gui's head to allow him to pull back. Royce keeps his left hand in front of the face to protect from the head butt.

6 Royce reaches inside his left sleeve with the right hand (fingers in and thumb out). He circles the left hand around and slips it under Gui's throat so the lower blade of the hand pushes up on the throat. Royce extends his legs to drive Gui back and extends his arms to tighten the sleeve choke on Gui's throat. The left hand pushes up into the throat and the right forearm presses down on the back of the neck for the submission.

109. Guard defense from punches: NHB Opponent stands up

Many times in a street fight or NHB match your opponent is able to get away from your guard and stand up, or he may be standing while you are on your back. In either case, Royce shows you how to react. Once again notice that in a street fight or NHB fight Royce is much more concerned about protecting himself than risking being struck in order to finish the fight. Throughout his history Royce has generally fought much bigger fighters and this strategy has served him well.

1 Gui stands in front of Royce and wants to punch him. Royce grabs both Gui's wrists with his hands and plants both feet on the hips so that his knees push down and out on Gui's elbows and forearms.

2 From that stance Royce has a variety of attack options. First he chooses the kick. While still holding Gui's wrists with his hands Royce coils his right leg back and thrusts it forward to hit Gui's face with the heel of his foot. Notice that to add power to the kick Royce pulls himself up by the hands (causing Gui to be pulled down into the kick as well). Royce can repeat this kick several times.

3 Royce can opt for the triangle right away instead of the kick or take advantage of Gui's disorientation after being struck and lock in the triangle. Royce pushes off his left leg and pulls himself up by the arms. He shoots his hips up and thrusts the right leg up and over Gui's head. Notice how Royce opens Gui's left arm wide to create more space for his leg to shoot through. Royce locks the right leg over Gui's head and completes the triangle by locking the left leg over the right foot to trap Gui's right arm and head.

110. Guard defense: NHB Opponent springs and leans forward

Another common situation from the guard is for the attacker to spring to his feet and lean forward while trying to throw punches. This time Royce does not want to take a chance on blocking or deflecting Gui's punch and quickly goes to a more controlling position. He may do that because his opponent is a terrific striker or much bigger than him.

1 Gui is in Royce's guard. Royce has good defensive position. His knees are on Gui's chest, the hands hold the back of Gui's arms and the forearms are blocking his biceps.

2 Royce quickly releases his knees from Gui's chest which causes him to fall forward. Royce closes the guard again and grabs Gui's head with the right arm and uses the left hand to protect his face from a head-butt.

3 Royce pushes Gui's head to the right with his left hand and slides the right arm on the right side of his head.

4 Royce re-locks his legs higher on Gui's back and grabs the right shin with both hands to push Gui's head down with the back of his right arm. Royce is in total control and Gui cannot punch him from here.

111. Guard defense: NHB Opponent springs and leans forward 2

Ideally Royce maintains control as he transitions to another position but at times his opponent may get an advantage. In this case Gui is able to free his arm and throws a punch. Again Royce first protects himself from being struck and then takes advantage of the attacker's weight commitment to secure a submission.

1 Gui is in Royce's guard and wants to strike. Royce has good defensive position. His knees are on Gui's chest, the hands hold the back of Gui's arms and the forearms block his biceps.

2 Gui manages to release his right arm, and is able to lean back, cock it and try to punch. Realizing he has temporarily lost of control over Gui's arms, Royce now needs to increase the distance between them. He pushes off his feet and drives his hips up to straighten his body and thrust his knees on Gui's chest to push him away. Now Gui's punches cannot hit Royce's face!

3 If Gui insists on striking, Royce can suddenly open his legs causing Gui to fall forward into his closed guard. Royce uses his left hand to push Gui's right arm across as he punches down and drives him to the right. Royce wraps the right arm around the left side of Gui's head. Notice that Gui's right arm and head are between Royce's arms now.

4 Royce bends the right arm over Gui's neck and locks the right hand on his left biceps. Royce bends the left arm and puts the hand on the right side of Gui's head. Royce now has a figure-4 head and arm triangle. He squeezes his elbows in for the choke. Royce adds power to the choke by pressing his head to the right as well.

112. Guard: Knee-through pass defense

The knee-through method is one of the strongest and most effective guard passes from standing. By sliding the knee between your legs he breaks your ability to apply a block with the leg. When that is coupled with the arm pulling your collar, it causes you to flatten your back on the ground. The attacker is in control and has most of the elements he needs to pass. Royce has a good answer to that problem.

1 Gui stands up in Royce's guard and breaks open his legs. Gui's right hand controls Royce's right collar while his left hand pushes down on Royce's right leg to create the opening. Gui points the right knee between Royce's legs.

2 Gui slides the right knee between Royce's legs and drives it over the right thigh while his right hand pulls on Royce's right lapel. Royce must act now or his guard will be passed. As soon as Gui begins to slide the right knee, Royce turns to his right and slides the left knee in front of Gui's hips. At the same time he locks the right foot on Gui's left thigh to block his path forward.

3 If Gui continues to persist in the pass, Royce will prop off his right elbow and push on Gui's back with his left hand to force him in the direction of his pass as he slips to the left. Gui may try to fight back and grab Royce's right sleeves with the left hand to force him flat on the mat.

4 Gui and Royce end up on their knees facing each other. Gui continues to hold onto Royce's right collar, so Royce grabs Gui's belt with his left hand and pulls him forward. At the same time he yanks his right arm back and pulls Gui's left arm with it to force him to fall forward. From here Royce can take Gui's back.

5 Alternatively Gui may try to push Royce's right leg down with the left hand to clear one of the blocks. As he does that Royce reaches with his left hand and grabs Gui's belt.

6 Royce pulls Gui by the belt to force him to fall forward while at the same time he turns to his knees. Royce steps out with the right leg and presses his chest on Gui's back in control.

113. Guard: Stacking guard pass defense Step 1

Another very solid and effective guard pass is the traditional stacking guard pass. In it the attacker controls the defender's legs and stacks them over his head as he chooses a side to pass. Quick action is the best solution. Do not wait for the opponent to have full control over your legs and hips or it may be much more difficult to counter. Royce demonstrates various stages of the counter.

1 Gui is inside Royce's closed guard. In perfect posture with his torso and head erect Gui raises his hips and slides the left arm inside Royce's legs and under the right leg. Gui wants to reach under the leg and grab the opposite collar to stack Royce's legs over his head.

2 *Key:* Don't let him grab the collar! Royce blocks Gui's left hand (the arm that is under his right leg) from reaching his collar to complete the hold of the pass. Royce uses the right hand to grab Gui's left wrist as soon as it comes outside the leg and locks it there.

3 Royce pushes Gui's left wrist out and forces the arm open. He drops his right leg on top of the arm to weigh it down. This is very important – otherwise Gui can still dip his body down and slide his shoulder under Royce's right leg and gain enough advantage to stack him.

4 Royce then coils his right leg and places the foot on Gui's left biceps and pushes it back. Royce can either stay in the open guard or slide the leg down and relock the feet to replace the closed guard.

114. Guard: Stacking guard pass defense Step 2

In the second step Royce is slower to react and Gui is able to reach the opposite collar which gives him a much stronger position to stack Royce.

1 Gui is able to grab Royce's left collar with the left hand and proceeds to raise his body so he can drive forward and stack Royce's left leg over his head.

2 Royce's line of defense is to break the grip by pushing Gui's hand away with both hands.

3 Once he breaks Gui's grip Royce keeps the left hand grip on the wrist, releases the right leg from Gui's head as he turns to his left and wraps the right arm around Gui's arm making sure to wrap above the elbow.

4 Royce locks the right hand onto his left wrist to secure the figure-4 around Gui's arm. Royce pushes off his legs, turning to his right, and drives Gui's left wrist clockwise to force it around the shoulder for the key-lock.

115. Guard: Stacking guard pass defense Step 3

In this case Royce is very late to react. Gui has secured the grip on the opposite collar. He leans forward and begins stacking Royce's right leg. If Royce doesn't react, Gui will continue his forward drive, push Royce's leg out of the way and reach side control. Notice that this is not Royce's desired reaction but rather a last resort to retain the guard.

1 Gui is attempting to pass Royce's guard by using the stacking method. This time he gets further ahead and is able to grab the opposite collar with the hand on the arm that is under Royce's leg. This gives him extra leverage for the stacking. Gui pushes off his feet and pulls the collar to force Royce's right leg back over himself. If Royce doesn't react Gui will pass his guard. Royce places his right hand under Gui's left elbow and the left hand grips the same forearm near the elbow.

2 Royce opens Gui's left elbow by pushing up with the right hand and pulling with the left. As Gui's elbow opens it gives Royce a little room to bend the right leg and turn it in so his knee slides under Gui's left arm in front of the biceps. As the arm opens out Royce releases his left hand from Gui's forearm and slides it under the arm to help create and maintain the space for his knee to slide. Notice that at the same time as he opens Gui's arm Royce plants and pushes off the left foot to slide his hips slightly to the left. This gives him a better angle for the knee to go in under the arm.

3 At this point Royce has broken Gui's powerful grip and stops the stack. He can choose to either loop the left leg over Gui's head and replace the guard or, as he does here, use both hands on Gui's left leg to block and pin him there as he continues to slide the hip left and drive his right leg under Gui's left arm.

4 Once his right leg emerges on Gui's right side, Royce pushes off his left foot and slides his hips back to center and replaces the guard.

116. Guard defense drill 1: Stacking guard standing

This drill is very good not only to practice the third step in the stacking guard defense but it is also very beneficial in developing important hip and leg movement. In addition it teaches you to learn to "give" instead of being stiff. The concept of giving instead of fighting power is very important in Gracie Jiu-Jitsu. For example, in the case of the third step defense of the stacking guard, if Royce fights the power by keeping his right leg stiff, it would only help Gui achieve his goal as Gui can continue driving his torso and use his power to force Royce's leg to stack over his body. But, since he is able to give and bend the leg under the pressure, he is able to regain his block. This same principle applies often, especially in guard defense and replacement.

Royce positions himself to start the drill with his back on the ground and Gui standing in front of him with his body erect. Royce's legs should be up and Gui's arms under them. Gui starts out by driving his right arm across pushing Royce's left leg towards the right. Royce "gives" – he bends the left leg at the knee. Royce slides the knee under Gui's right arm and loops the foot around it until it clears. As soon as that happens Gui twists his torso to the left and uses his left arm to drive Royce's right leg in the same direction. Royce once again gives into the power and bends the right leg in so his knee slides under Gui's left arm. He loops the foot around the arm and ends up in the neutral starting stance. Continue with this motion back and forth; as you begin to master the movement have your partner increase the speed and increase the pressure. Always try to keep your hips up and slightly off the ground to give you more space to move them and increase your speed. As you practice this drill it is common and even desirable to slide away from the opponent slightly, so repeat it up and down the mat.

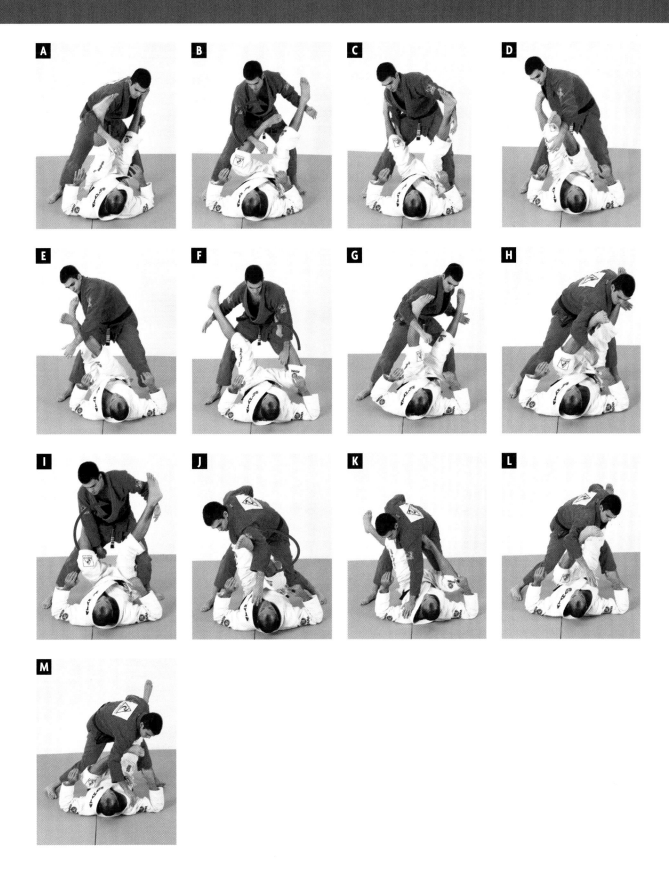

117. Guard defense drill 2: Stacking guard kneeling

This drill is the same as the previous except the opponent is kneeling, which creates more difficulty for your movement. It also forces you to loosen up the hips: a very important mechanics in defending the guard.

Royce positions himself to start the drill with his back on the ground and Gui kneeling in front of him with his body erect. Royce's legs should be up and Gui's arms under them. Gui starts out driving his right arm across to push Royce's left leg towards the right. Royce gives and bends the left leg at the knee. He slides the knee under Gui's right arm and loops the foot around it until it clears. As soon as that happens Gui twists his torso to the right. He uses his left arm to drive Royce's right leg to his left. Royce once again gives into the power and

bends the right leg in so his knee slides under Gui's left arm and loops the foot around it to end up in the neutral starting stance. Continue with this motion back and forth; as you begin to master the movement have your partner increase the speed and then increase the pressure. Always try to keep your hips up and slightly off the ground to give you more space to move them and increase your speed. As you practice this drill it is common and even desirable to slide away from the opponent slightly so repeat it up and down the mat.

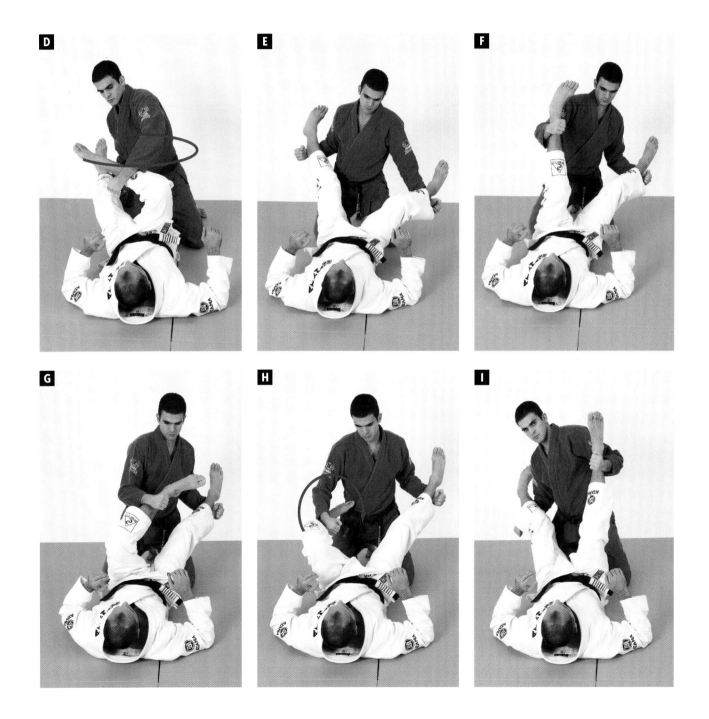

118. Guard defense drill 3:
Stacking guard more pressure

This drill goes one step further than the previous ones. Once you've mastered the first two drills, then advance to this one. This time you allow the passer to reach a more advanced position in the pass, which forces you to use more of your body to replace the guard. Aside from teaching you to move your hips and legs and learning the concept of "giving", this drill also teaches you to use your feet to move your body and bring the coordination of your legs, arms, hips and torso into one effective movement.

Royce positions himself to start the drill with his back on the ground and Gui kneeling in front of him. Royce's legs should be up and Gui's arms under them. In this case Royce's hips are on the ground and not up as in the previous drill. This makes it more difficult for him to execute the movement so he has to engage the use of his feet and legs to help move the hips and torso from side to side. Gui starts the drill by driving his torso forward and to his right to stack Royce's right leg over his body. Gui's arm under the leg reaches further across Royce's side than in the previous drill. Royce places his right hand on Gui's left hip and the left one on his shoulder to block his pass slightly. Royce steps out with the left leg and pushes off it to escape the hips to the left and turn his torso to the

right. As the hip escapes to the opposite side, Royce's front knee drops in front and under Gui's left arm. He then loops the left leg over Gui's head and rests it on the left shoulder. Royce makes sure that his right foot hooks the outside of Gui's right hip. Now he has replaced the guard and keeps Gui from going to either side by first using his right foot to stop the movement to the left and then the left leg to block Gui's movement to the right. At this point Gui starts passing to the other side as his head is on the proper side of the top leg (in this case, the left leg). Repeat the movement up and down the mat and intensify the pressure as you master the technique.

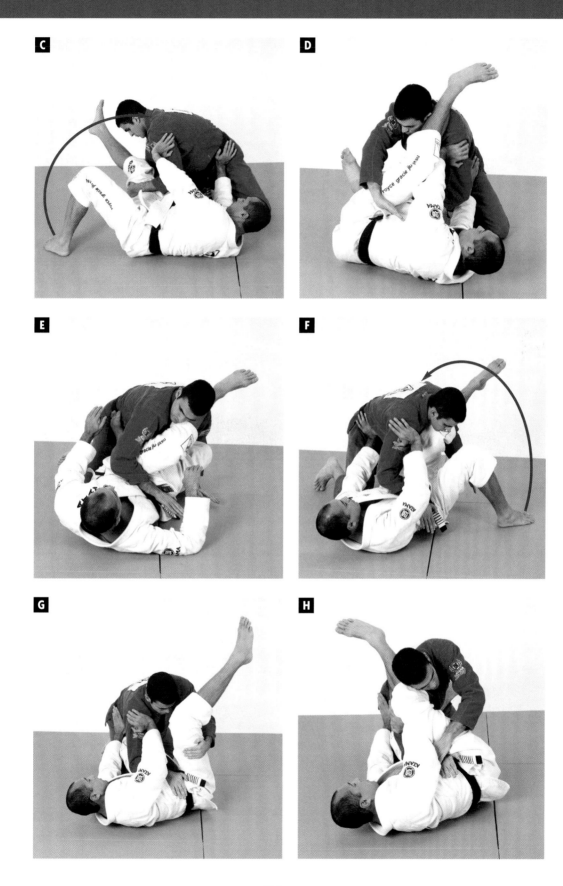

119. Guard defense drill 4: Leg swing and block

In this drill you will learn to use the leg swing to move your body and to block the opponent's passing as he switches from one side to the other. The leg swing is very important as it is used not only in guard defense but also in some sweeps, arm-locks and to create space in certain situations. Mastering the proper swing and learning how to connect the power of the swing with your body will amplify your ability to apply many moves.

Royce starts the drill on his side with the right knee and shin in front of Gui's hips. His left leg is over Gui's head and rests on his left shoulder. Royce's right hand pushes on Gui's left hip and the left hand pushes on the shoulder. Gui is kneeling with his torso leaning forward to apply pressure on Royce's left leg. Gui starts the drill by reaching with his right arm to grab Royce's right collar with the hand as he tries to pass to Royce's left. Royce swings the left leg over Gui's head to the left and uses the back of his thigh to block Gui's right arm and the hand from grabbing the collar. The leg swing also made

Royce's hips move to the right and centered his body. Gui then tries to go back to Royce's right side; Royce swings the left leg back over Gui's head and to the right. He locks the leg over Gui's left shoulder and blocks the pass to that side. The leg swing to the right helps Royce's hips escape to the left. Repeat the drill back and forth and increase the speed and then the pressure as you master the movement. If your opponent gets too tight on you make use of the teeter-totter to create space as you push off the legs and escape the body up and away.

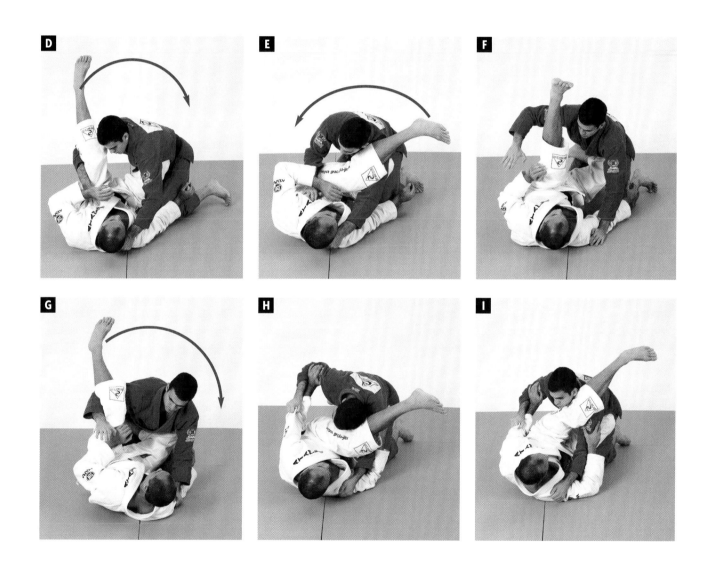

120. Guard defense drill 5:
Stacking guard step 4 & Drill roll over and back

This drill develops several skills at the same time. It develops your ability to roll back and forward under pressure, along with your awareness of when a position is lost. It also develops the concept of pushing and giving.

This is the fourth step in the stacking guard defense. When everything appears to be lost and the passer has full control over your leg and is stacking you, use the roll over and back to recover the guard!

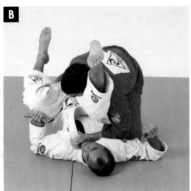

Royce begins the drill with his back on the ground and the right leg up on Gui's left shoulder. Gui grabs Royce's left collar with his left hand and pushes off his feet to drive forward with his torso. This forces Royce's right leg back and stacks him. Royce needs to time the movement perfectly as he wants to take advantage of Gui's forward pressure to roll over his shoulder. The first thing he does is to push back with the right leg against Gui's shoulder as if he was fighting the stack. When Gui pushes forward he uses that momentum to extend the body and use the pressure of the leg to roll over his outside (left) shoulder

and get to the knees. Royce escapes the head under Gui's left arm. He steps out with the left leg and pushes off the foot as he continues to roll back. Royce drops the right leg on the ground and thrusts his head back, using it to push Gui's left arm so he falls forward. Royce replaces the guard. Royce gets back to the original position except this time Gui uses the right arm under Royce's leg and repeats the motion to the opposite side. It is very important for Royce to take advantage of Gui's forward pressure against his leg and use it to help him roll backwards over the shoulder.